THE
WORLD
PUZZLE
CHAMPIONSHIP
CHALLENGE

Dr Gareth Moore is the author of over 100 puzzle and brain-training books for both children and adults, including *The Mammoth Book of Logical Brain Games*, *The Mindfulness Puzzle Book* and *The Mammoth Book of New Sudoku*. His puzzles also appear in a range of newspapers and magazines.

He is also the creator of the daily brain-training website *BrainedUp.com*, and runs popular puzzle site *PuzzleMix.com*.

THE
WORLD
PUZZLE
CHAMPIONSHIP
CHALLENGE

DR GARETH MOORE

ROBINSON

ROBINSON

First published in Great Britain in 2018 by Robinson

1 3 5 7 9 10 8 6 4 2

Copyright © Dr Gareth Moore, 2018
Puzzles copyright © World Puzzle Federation 2008-2017

A CIP catalogue record for this book
is available from the British Library.

ISBN: 978-1-47214-268-9

Typeset in Minion Pro by Dr Gareth Moore
Printed and bound in Great Britain by CPI Group (UK), Croydon
CRO 4YY

Papers used by Robinson are from well-managed forests and other
responsible sources.

Robinson
An imprint of
Little, Brown Book Group
Carmelite House
50 Victoria Embankment
London EC4Y 0DZ

An Hachette UK Company
www.hachette.co.uk

www.littlebrown.co.uk

CONTENTS

Prelude

Individual Puzzle Types

World Puzzle Championship Rounds

Solutions

For puzzlers everywhere

INTRODUCTION

Every autumn, some of the brightest minds from around the globe gather for a multi-day event called the World Puzzle Championship (WPC). Its purpose is to determine who is the best puzzle solver in the world – using puzzles that are language- and culture-neutral, so everyone can compete equally, no matter what their native tongue or background. Crosswords and other word puzzles are not included.

The first WPC, held in New York in 1992, was attended by teams from twelve countries. The event has grown to dozens of countries today and moves to a different city each year – London, Amsterdam, Prague, Istanbul, Beijing, Bangalore, Rio de Janeiro, and elsewhere.

Some of the puzzles in the WPC forecast future puzzle trends. For example, sudoku was introduced at the championship years before it became an international craze. Other varieties of puzzle that are popular with WPC contestants remain little known, at least for now.

This book consists of just under 200 former WPC puzzles, arranged in 16 chapters by type – Cave, Slitherlink, Tents, etc. Each one includes some standard puzzles of that type along with a few variants. The last three chapters consist of full rounds from a previous WPC, so (if you wish) you can compare your times against the 'best in the world' and see how you do.

However you approach this book, whether competitively or just for fun, your mind will be stretched.

Happy solving!

Will Shortz
Founder, World Puzzle Championship
Chairman, World Puzzle Federation

INSTRUCTIONS
HOW TO USE THIS BOOK

Welcome to *The World Puzzle Championship Challenge: Are You as Bright as the Best?*

Packed from cover to cover with a huge range of puzzles, this book contains almost 200 of the puzzles that have been used to test the world's brightest and best puzzle solvers over the past ten years or so – as well as dozens and dozens of further puzzles that are provided as examples.

To help make sense of the huge number of puzzles, the content is broken down into 20 sections. The first 16 each introduce a particular puzzle, while chapters 17, 18 and 19 each contain a complete round from a recent World Puzzle Championship (WPC), along with the results of the best solvers at that tournament, so you can compare your own performance and answer the title question: 'Are you as bright as the best?'. Finally, chapter 20 contains solutions to all of the puzzles in the book.

At the bottom of every page with a puzzle on, you'll see a note of which WPC tournament, which round of that tournament, and which question within that round the puzzle came from.

Individual Puzzle Chapters
Chapters 1 to 16 each focus on a particular type of puzzle. Each of these chapters begins with a page of instructions, along with an example puzzle and its solution. Use the example to make sure you understand the rules of the puzzle, by working out how the rules as given fit the

INSTRUCTIONS

solution, and to work out what exactly it is you need to do to solve that particular puzzle.

Sometimes the rules may sound complex, but the concepts are always relatively straightforward and so the example pictures will usually help to resolve any confusion that the written instructions might lead to. You can also try solving the example, comparing your progress against the solution as you go.

The instructions are then followed by a few examples of the puzzle as described, taken directly from previous WPC competitions. Each puzzle is presented in exactly the same way as it was given to the on-site competitors, so that you can experience the puzzles in their true original form. This does mean that there are sometimes minor changes in appearance, such as changes in grid style or in the appearance of certain elements, but you should ignore these – the core rules always remain the same, unless specifically otherwise stated on the page.

Talking of rule changes, each chapter also includes a number of 'variant' puzzles, which are identified by additional text beneath the puzzle. This usually says 'Extra Instructions', and then includes a description of what makes that variant different to the usual version of the puzzle. Unless the variation is very straightforward, it is also accompanied by a new example solution (and usually an example puzzle too) to help you fully understand the new instructions.

Each year, at the WPC, puzzle authors like to come up with new variations on existing puzzles to provide new challenges for that year's solvers – by trying the variants in this book, you'll be experiencing the challenges that this brings for yourself. It's often fascinating how even a small change in the rules for a puzzle can result in a very different solving experience.

INSTRUCTIONS

World Puzzle Championship Round Chapters

Chapters 17, 18 and 19 are something special. Each of these chapters includes a complete round from a previous WPC, presented exactly as the original competitors saw it. The only changes are to format the rounds for the page size of this book, and to very slightly modify the instructions for consistency of phrasing. The actual competition puzzles, and all of the example puzzles, too, are the exact ones that appeared in the original events.

Each of these chapters starts with a page that introduces the particular round, and then is followed by the 'instruction book' for that round. This corresponds with the instructions for the actual WPC, which are released before the competition so that competitors can understand the rules for a puzzle in advance. Then, when they come to the actual competition, they are ready to solve the puzzles without needing to work out what the instructions are.

Typically, WPC instructions are published only around a week before the competition, so competitors don't have too long to practise. Another reason that the instruction books are released in advance of the competition is so that those competitors who do not have English as a first language (which is the vast majority) have a chance to make sense of the instructions. While the actual puzzles are always intended to be solvable by anyone from anywhere in the world, the instructions are always provided in English.

For each of these three chapters, then, start by reading the 'instruction book' and using the example puzzles and solutions to understand the rules. Once you think you are fully prepared, you can – if you wish – then time yourself completing the puzzles in the round, and see how you fare against the result of the best solver that year. Alternatively, you could of course treat these chapters as any other in the book, and simply solve each puzzle at your leisure. It's up to you.

INSTRUCTIONS

Solutions Chapter

The final chapter contains the complete solution to every full-page puzzle – all of the examples have their solutions alongside them within the book. Solutions are referenced by page number, to avoid confusion.

You can of course use the solutions to check your answers, but you can also use them to make the puzzles easier. If you get stuck on a puzzle, you could take a quick look at the solution and see if that gets you going. You could also copy some extra clues from the solution back into the puzzle, to help. These puzzles are aimed at the best in the world, so there's no shame in simplifying them a little!

Solving Hints

Learning by experimentation is often the best way to get going on an unfamiliar puzzle. Try anything, and see what happens. Once it contradicts the rules, you might notice something about the puzzle that gives you a hint as to how to go about solving it with a little less guesswork. A good example is the puzzle slitherlink, featured in chapter 14. If you were to sit and try to think logically about how to go about solving it, you might find it rather intimidating – but if you just pick up your pencil and get cracking, you might well discover that you make deductions it would have taken you much longer to uncover by just sitting and staring at the unsolved grid.

Use a pencil for solving, and don't be afraid to grab an eraser and rub the whole thing out and start again if you need to. Another tip is to mark in not just what you know is right, but also what you know is wrong. This might for example be done by placing small 'x's in the grid.

Most of all, remember to stop once you aren't having fun. Come back the next day, or try a different puzzle.

Dr Gareth Moore
Email: gareth@drgarethmoore.com / Twitter: @drgarethmoore

THE UK TEAM
COULD YOU QUALIFY?

Every year, the UK Puzzle Association (UKPA) organises qualifying competitions to select a team of the four best UK solvers for the World Puzzle Championship. The UKPA also selects a team for that year's World Sudoku Championship, which typically takes place immediately before the World Puzzle Championship.

Most years we select not just an A team but also a B team for each event, and sometimes also a C team. Only A team members are eligible to win the world title, but the whole squad has a fantastic team spirit, with everyone equal outside the competition hall.

The UKPA organises an Open competition weekend each year, where British solvers come to compete with one another both for team selection and for fun. The puzzles are of a similar standard and variety to those found at the World Puzzle Championship, and grouped into rounds just like at the actual competition. There are enough puzzles to keep everyone of every ability busy for the full duration, and the big bonus of this event is meeting others with the same interest and skills. Often people find they have other things in common, too, and many friendships are formed here.

Every June, we also hold an online UK championship for each event. This allows everyone another chance to qualify, including those who were unable to make the on-site Open earlier in the year.

If you'd like to take part in either competition, visit www.ukpuzzles.org – where there are also details on how each team is chosen. Could you be in next year's team?

THE UK TEAM

The UKPA also provides a puzzle-discussion forum that is free for everyone, and is full of useful puzzle links, tips and ideas. Whatever your level, age, nationality or background, you are very welcome. The very best solvers will also be invited to join as a full member of a very exclusive club, where everything you need to succeed at the highest level is available to you.

The UKPA is the British member of the World Puzzle Federation (WPF). Like the WPF itself, it is a non-profit organisation, run by and for competitors, with no financial reward for its organisers. We welcome and encourage puzzle solvers of all abilities, so don't be shy. If you enjoy the puzzles in this book, please do drop by to say hello, or ask a question.

Alan O'Donnell
Chairman, UK Puzzle Association

1.
BATTLESHIPS

BATTLESHIPS
INSTRUCTIONS

In this puzzle, the aim is to place a given fleet of ships into a grid – but in such a way that none of the ships touches another, not even diagonally.

Clues outside the grid show the number of occupied squares in the corresponding row or column. Ships cannot be in a square with a wave symbol. Some ship segments from the solution may also be given, as shown in the example below.

In some puzzles, there may be rows or columns without clues. This means that you don't know anything about them – they may or may not be empty.

Example   **Solution**

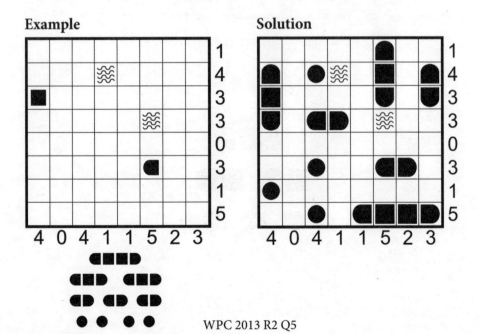

WPC 2013 R2 Q5

BATTLESHIPS
PUZZLE 1

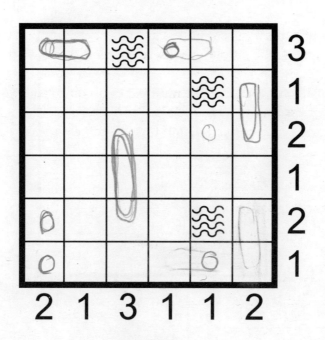

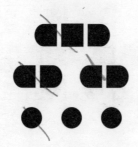

WPC 2011 R14 Q7

BATTLESHIPS
PUZZLE 2

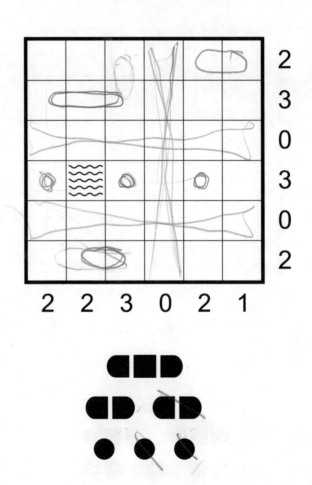

WPC 2010 R2 Q1

Instructions on page 16

BATTLESHIPS
PUZZLE 3

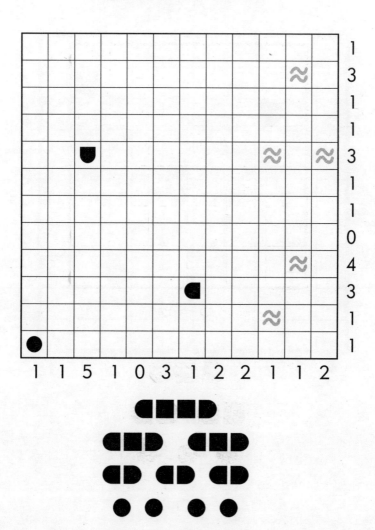

WPC 2012 R5 Q2

BATTLESHIPS
PUZZLE 4

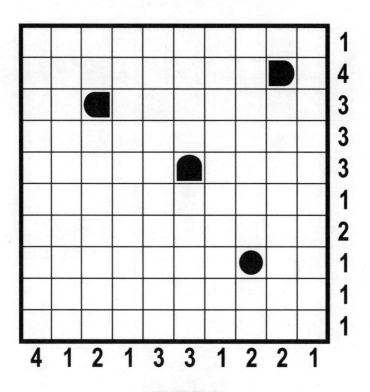

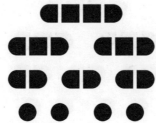

WPC 2011 R16 Q2

Instructions on page 16

BATTLESHIPS
PUZZLE 5

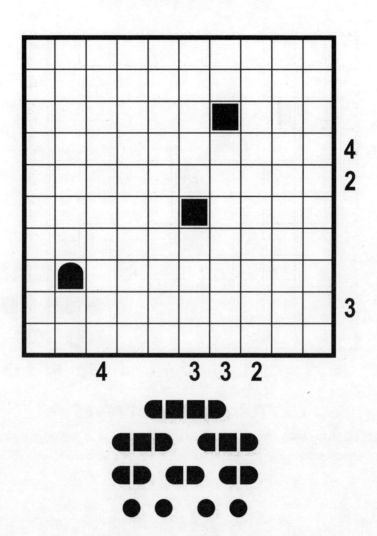

WPC 2011 R2 Q1

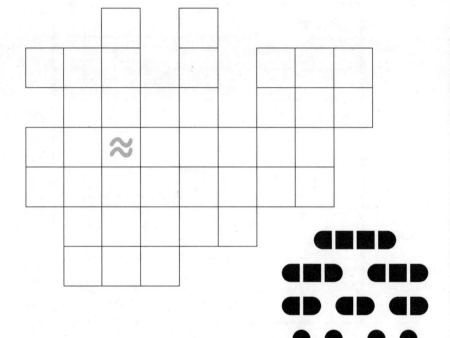

EXTRA INSTRUCTIONS

Place all 10 ships into this differently shaped grid. No number clues are necessary because the grid shape forces a unique solution.

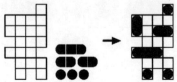

WPC 2012 R10 Q15

Instructions on page 16

BATTLESHIPS
SEA BY NUMBERS

			1		1	3	
			2		2	1	
			4		3	1	

2 1 2

1 4 1

1 1 1

EXTRA INSTRUCTIONS

The clue digits now reveal the length (in squares) of every region of empty sea in the given row or column, in order from left-to-right or top-to-bottom.

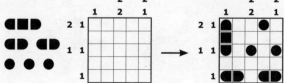

WPC 2008 R7 Q7

BATTLESHIPS
SHIPS IN FORMATION 1

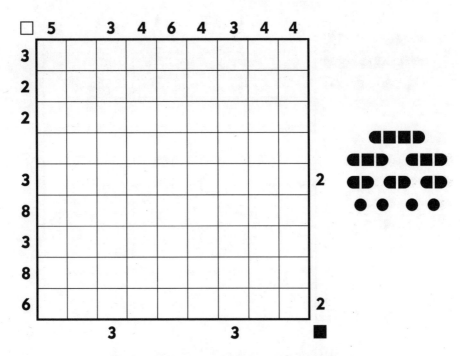

EXTRA INSTRUCTIONS

Numbers below and to the right of the grid indicate the longest sequence of black squares (occupied by ships) in the corresponding row/column. Numbers above and to the left of the grid indicate the longest sequence of white squares (not occupied by ships) in the corresponding row/column.

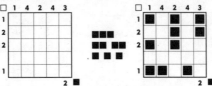

WPC 2012 R8 Q9

Instructions on page 16

BATTLESHIPS
SHIPS IN FORMATION 2

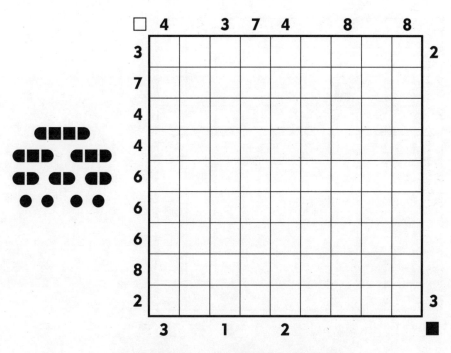

EXTRA INSTRUCTIONS

Numbers below and to the right of the grid indicate the longest sequence of black squares (occupied by ships) in the corresponding row/column. Numbers above and to the left of the grid indicate the longest sequence of white squares (not occupied by ships) in the corresponding row/column.

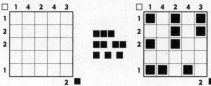

WPC 2012 R8 Q10

BATTLESHIPS
COLLIDING SHIPS

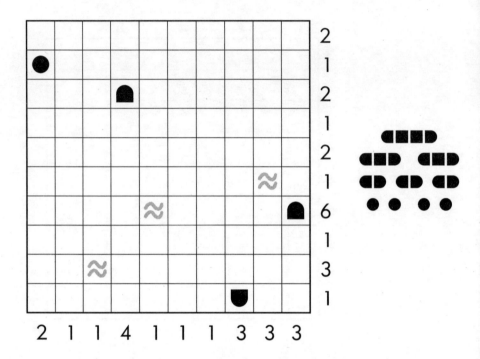

EXTRA INSTRUCTIONS

Normal rules apply, except that exactly two ships will be touching. These two ships must be of different sizes.

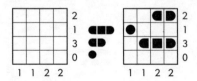

WPC 2012 R3 Q10

Instructions on page 16

2.
CAVE

INSTRUCTIONS

Form a single 'cave' of connected squares by shading the squares outside the cave, so every unshaded square is inside the cave. Numbered squares must remain unshaded. All squares in the cave must be connected by at least one side.

Each numbered square reveals the total number of visible squares (from the point of view of that number) within the cave and in the same row or column, including the numbered square itself. A square is visible from a number if there is no unshaded square between it and the number in the same row or column.

All squares outside the cave must be connected to the edge of the grid. Squares are considered to be connected if they share a side.

Example

		5		2		
	3				3	
2		9		5		5
			4			
8		11		7		8
	4				4	
		2		2		

Solution

		5		2		
	3				3	
2		9		5		5
			4			
8		11		7		8
	4				4	
		2		2		

WPC 2011 R2 Q14

CAVE
PUZZLE 1

			6						
	3							2	
				4		6			
		4							4
					4		4		
		5		3					
6							3		
			2		6				
	3							2	
						6			

WPC 2016 R9 Q14

CAVE
PUZZLE 2

		3		4		5		3
	2		7		5		6	
7				7				5
	4		9		7		4	
9		9		9		9		

WPC 2017 R3 Q21

Instructions on page 28

CAVE
PUZZLE 3

		7					
	5					3	
		6			7		7
			4		6		
			7		6		
7		4			5		
	6					2	
					7		

WPC 2017 R3 Q22

CAVE
PUZZLE 4

2						2
		2		2		
2						
		2				
2				2		
2			2		2	

WPC 2013 R9 Q3

Instructions on page 28

CAVE
PUZZLE 5

			3				
		3		3			3
	3					3	
3				3			3
			3				
	3			3			
3					3		
				3		3	

WPC 2013 R9 Q3

CAVE
PUZZLE 6

		4					4
	4						
4			4				
		4				4	
4			4				4
				4			
		4					4
4						4	

WPC 2013 R9 Q3

Instructions on page 28

CAVE
PUZZLE 7

			5		5			5	
							5		
		5		5		5		5	
							5		
5		5				5			
			5						5
		5						5	
	5		5		5				
		5							
								5	

WPC 2016 R2 Q5

CAVE
FULL CAVE

2	4	6	2	4	3	6	4
7	5	3	4	7	5	5	2
5	4	8	6	3	2	5	8
4	6	5	2	5	6	4	2
7	4	4	7	8	6	5	4
4	4	2	5	3	6	3	3
3	5	5	8	6	5	6	7
5	3	2	5	3	4	2	9

EXTRA INSTRUCTIONS

Shade squares so that those that remain make a valid cave solution.

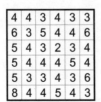 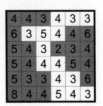

WPC 2016 R4 Q4

Instructions on page 28

3.

DOMINOES

DOMINOES
INSTRUCTIONS

A given set of dominoes has been placed into the grid, with exactly one of each domino. Draw along the lines to mark the position of each domino.

Example

4	6	2	5	5	2	0	1
0	4	4	0	0	1	6	3
2	4	4	1	1	3	1	5
2	5	0	2	2	2	0	0
5	3	3	6	4	1	3	5
1	4	1	4	5	6	6	5
6	6	3	0	3	3	6	2

Solution

4	6	2	5	5	2	0	1
0	4	4	0	0	1	6	3
2	4	4	1	1	3	1	5
2	5	0	2	2	2	0	0
5	3	3	6	4	1	3	5
1	4	1	4	5	6	6	5
6	6	3	0	3	3	6	2

0-0
0-1 1-1
0-2 1-2 2-2
0-3 1-3 2-3 3-3
0-4 1-4 2-4 3-4 4-4
0-5 1-5 2-5 3-5 4-5 5-5
0-6 1-6 2-6 3-6 4-6 5-6 6-6

WPC 2014 instruction booklet

DOMINOES
PUZZLE 1

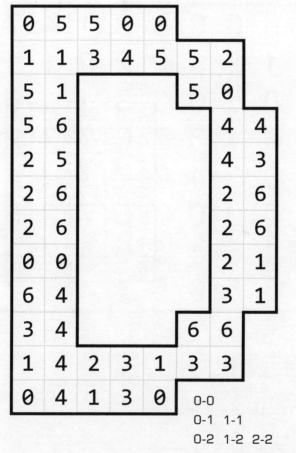

0	5	5	0	0			
1	1	3	4	5	5	2	
5	1				5	0	
5	6					4	4
2	5					4	3
2	6					2	6
2	6					2	6
0	0					2	1
6	4					3	1
3	4				6	6	
1	4	2	3	1	3	3	
0	4	1	3	0			

```
0-0
0-1  1-1
0-2  1-2  2-2
0-3  1-3  2-3  3-3
0-4  1-4  2-4  3-4  4-4
0-5  1-5  2-5  3-5  4-5  5-5
0-6  1-6  2-6  3-6  4-6  5-6  6-6
```

WPC 2017 R12 Q4

DOMINOES
PUZZLE 2

4	5	5	6	6	3	1	4	7
6	1	2	3	2	2	2	1	1
1	0	0	0	3	3	1	1	6
6	0	4	3	7	6	7	3	2
6	0	2	4	7	7	7	2	1
1	0	0	0	7	5	7	2	3
3	4	5	4	5	5	4	2	6
0	3	5	6	5	4	4	5	7

0 0	1 1	2 2	3 3	4 4	5 5	6 6	7 7
0 1	1 2	2 3	3 4	4 5	5 6	6 7	
0 2	1 3	2 4	3 5	4 6	5 7		
0 3	1 4	2 5	3 6	4 7			
0 4	1 5	2 6	3 7				
0 5	1 6	2 7					
0 6	1 7						
0 7							

WPC 2013 R7 Q9

Instructions on page 38

DOMINOES
DEFICIENT DOMINOES

0	0	1	1	2	3	3	5	4	0
3	3	2	5	6	6	3	4	2	0
6	3	0	6	1	1	6	4	2	0
2	2	4	3	6	6	1	3	2	2
2	4	4	0	0	5	4	5	5	5
1	1	4	6	0	5	1	3	5	3

```
0-0
0-1 1-1
0-2 1-2 2-2
0-3 1-3 2-3 3-3
0-4 1-4 2-4 3-4 4-4
0-5 1-5 2-5 3-5 4-5 5-5
0-6 1-6 2-6 3-6 4-6 5-6 6-6
```

EXTRA INSTRUCTIONS

Some numbers in the grid are left over, and not used by any domino tile.

	1	3	0	1	2
3	2	2	0	0	3
1	1	1	3	3	2
1	0	2	0	0	

```
0-0
0-1 1-1
0-2 1-2 2-2
0-3 1-3 2-3 3-3
```

	1	3	0	1	2
3	2	2	0	0	3
1	1	1	3	3	2
1	0	2	0	0	

WPC 2012 R3 Q4

DOMINOES
DOMINO HUNT 1

0	0	1	0		0	1	5	
1	6	3	3	2	1	4	3	2	6
4	6	4	0			4	5	5	4
	2	3					6	0	5
1	2	4	3			2	4		2
3	0	3	2		6	0	5	1	1
		6	6	4	5	6	5		

```
0-0
0-1  1-1
0-2  1-2  2-2
0-3  1-3  2-3  3-3
0-4  1-4  2-4  3-4  4-4
0-5  1-5  2-5  3-5  4-5  5-5
0-6  1-6  2-6  3-6  4-6  5-6  6-6
```

EXTRA INSTRUCTIONS

Some numbers in the grid have been erased, and must be restored.

WPC 2012 R14 Q1

Instructions on page 38

DOMINOES
DOMINO HUNT 2

3	6			0	1	1	3	0	1	5	5
6	2			0	4	5		6	1	6	2
0	4		0	6	5	6	1		3		
0	2	3	5	2	2	3	3				
6	4	2	4	4	3	5	2		5	0	1
	1			4					1	4	2

```
0-0
0-1  1-1
0-2  1-2  2-2
0-3  1-3  2-3  3-3
0-4  1-4  2-4  3-4  4-4
0-5  1-5  2-5  3-5  4-5  5-5
0-6  1-6  2-6  3-6  4-6  5-6  6-6
```

EXTRA INSTRUCTIONS

Some numbers in the grid have been erased, and must be restored.

	0	3		1	5			
	2	4	3	4	6			
	3	6	0	5	4	6	4	4
3	6	2	3	6	6	1	5	6
3	5	1	2	0	5	2	3	6
4	2	4	1	1	3	5	2	1
	0	1	1	2	2			
	0	5		4	0			

	0	3	0	1	5			
	2	4	3	4	6			
0	3	6	0	5	4	6	4	4
3	6	2	3	6	6	1	5	6
3	5	1	2	0	5	2	3	6
4	2	4	1	1	3	5	2	1
	0	1	1	2	2			
	0	5	5	4	0			

WPC 2012 R1 Q1

DOMINOES
DOMINO CASTLE 1

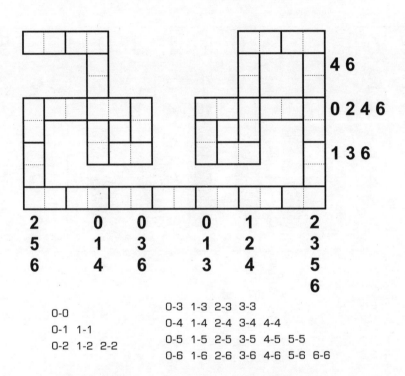

4 6

0 2 4 6

1 3 6

2 0 0 0 1 2
5 1 3 1 2 3
6 4 6 3 4 5
        6

0-0

0-1 1-1

0-2 1-2 2-2

0-3 1-3 2-3 3-3

0-4 1-4 2-4 3-4 4-4

0-5 1-5 2-5 3-5 4-5 5-5

0-6 1-6 2-6 3-6 4-6 5-6 6-6

EXTRA INSTRUCTIONS

Place each domino exactly once. Halves of dominoes sharing a side must contain the same numbers. Numbers outside the grid indicate <u>all</u> of the numbers that are used in the corresponding direction, in any order.

WPC 2009 R3 Q6

DOMINOES
DOMINO CASTLE 2

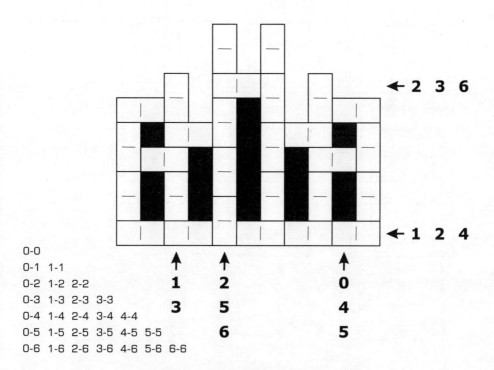

← 2 3 6

← 1 2 4

0-0
0-1 1-1
0-2 1-2 2-2
0-3 1-3 2-3 3-3
0-4 1-4 2-4 3-4 4-4
0-5 1-5 2-5 3-5 4-5 5-5
0-6 1-6 2-6 3-6 4-6 5-6 6-6

↑ 1   ↑ 2   ↑ 0
  3   5   4
  6   5

EXTRA INSTRUCTIONS

Place each domino exactly once. Halves of dominoes sharing a side must contain the same numbers. Numbers outside the grid indicate <u>all</u> of the numbers that are used in the corresponding direction, in any order.

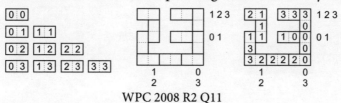

WPC 2008 R2 Q11

DOMINOES
DOMINO CASTLE 3

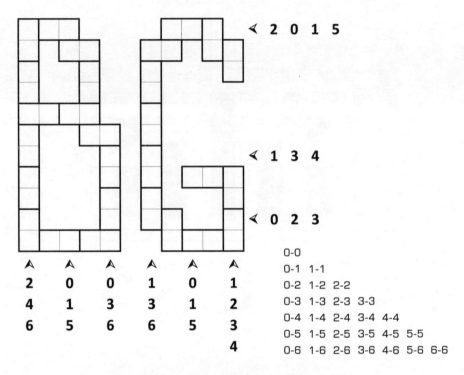

```
0-0
0-1  1-1
0-2  1-2  2-2
0-3  1-3  2-3  3-3
0-4  1-4  2-4  3-4  4-4
0-5  1-5  2-5  3-5  4-5  5-5
0-6  1-6  2-6  3-6  4-6  5-6  6-6
```

EXTRA INSTRUCTIONS

Place each domino exactly once. Halves of dominoes sharing a side must contain the same numbers. Numbers outside the grid indicate <u>all</u> of the numbers that are used in the corresponding direction, in any order.

WPC 2015 R12 Q2

Instructions on page 38

4.

FILLOMINO

FILLOMINO
INSTRUCTIONS

Fill each empty square with a number so that every number in the grid is part of a continuous region of that many squares. A region is continuous whenever two squares touch by a side.

Two different regions made up of the same number of squares cannot touch by a side.

Example

	5						1	
	7						2	
		7		7		5		
		5		5				
	7						3	
	6		3			7		
		5		5				
1	2		4		4		2	1
			3					

Solution

7	5	5	5	5	7	7	1	5
7	7	5	7	7	7	2	2	5
6	7	7	5	7	7	5	5	5
6	7	8	5	3	5	3	3	4
6	7	8	5	3	5	5	3	4
6	6	8	5	3	5	7	7	4
6	2	8	5	4	5	7	2	4
1	2	8	4	4	4	7	2	1
8	8	8	3	3	3	7	7	7

WPC 2017 R14 Q1

FILLOMINO
PUZZLE 1

	3	5		5	4		4	4	
1									6
3									3
			2	6	2	6			
6			6			2			1
1			2			6			2
			6	2	6	2			
3									5
2									6
	3	4		4	6		2	1	

WPC 2017 R14 Q2

FILLOMINO
PUZZLE 2

1	2	3	4	5	6	7	8		8
									8
2								8	
	8		8				8		8
1		7				7		2	
	8								3
8									
1		8	7	6	5	4	3	2	1

WPC 2016 R9 Q15

Instructions on page 48

FILLOMINO
PUZZLE 3

1	5	6	2	2	6	3	1
9							4
5	5	3	4	4	2	2	7
7	2	7	5	4	3	6	3
9							7
9	5	4	8	6	6	2	2

WPC 2016 R9 Q16

FILLOMINO
RESTRICTED

2		2	4		2		4
							2
3		2		2		2	3
						3	2
3		3		3			
			4			4	4
2	4						
	4	2		2		2	4
2							
	3		2		3		2	2

EXTRA INSTRUCTIONS

All different polyomino sizes used in the grid are given (so in this puzzle regions can only be of sizes 2, 3 or 4, or in the example of sizes 3 or 13).

	13		3	
3				13
13				13
	13		3	

3	13	3	3	3
3	13	13	13	13
3	13	3	3	3
13	13	13	13	13
13	13	3	3	3

WPC 2017 R14 Q5

Instructions on page 48

FILLOMINO
NONCONSECUTIVE

5							
	1		4				21
			20	20			
	4	20					
		20					
						22	
						22	3
				22	22		
	21					6	5
							7

EXTRA INSTRUCTIONS

Two adjacent squares must not contain consecutive numbers (i.e. must not contain a difference of 1). They *can* touch diagonally, however.

			5	
5				1
		6		
4				
	3		2	

5	5	5	3	5	5
5	1	5	3	5	1
1	4	1	3	5	5
4	4	6	6	2	2
4	1	3	6	6	6
1	3	3	6	2	2

WPC 2017 R14 Q4

FILLOMINO
SUM

EXTRA INSTRUCTIONS

The number at the top left of each cage gives the sum of all numbers that appear inside it.

WPC 2017 R14 Q6

Instructions on page 48

FILLOMINO

QUEEN

	2	6			2		2		
			13				3	2	
	8					5	3		
8			1		2	5			
	6			2	2			4	
			3	4					
2			3	4			4		
		2	3			4		2	
	4		2			3			
3		4			2				
	3			2			1	7	

EXTRA INSTRUCTIONS

No two 1-square regions can be in the same horizontal, vertical or diagonal line of squares. (Or, if '1's are considered as chess queens, then no queen can be threatening any other).

WPC 2017 R14 Q3

FILLOMINO
INSTRUCTIONLESS

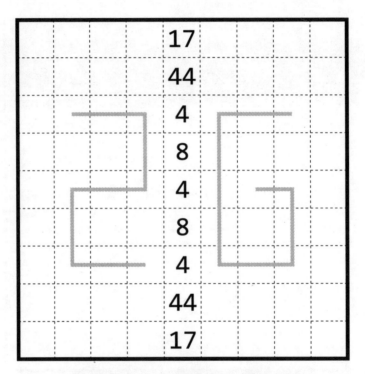

			17		
			44		
			4		
			8		
			4		
			8		
			4		
			44		
			17		

EXTRA INSTRUCTIONS

It is up to you to use this solved example to work out the extra rules:

1	2	4	6		
2			3		
4			2		
2	1	3	6		

3	3	2	4	4	4
3	1	2	4	6	6
2	2	3	3	3	6
4	4	4	2	2	6
4	2	1	3	6	6
1	2	3	3	2	2

WPC 2017 R14 Q7

Instructions on page 48

5.
HEYAWAKE

HEYAWAKE
INSTRUCTIONS

Shade some squares, so that no two shaded squares touch by a side, and all unshaded squares form a single continuous area.

Numbered squares may or may not be shaded, but always give the precise amount of shaded squares in their bold-lined region.

Any continuous horizontal or vertical line of unshaded squares cannot cross more than one bold line.

Example

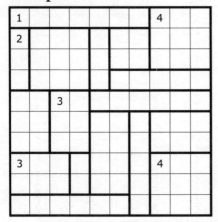

Solution

WPC 2015 R2 Q14

HEYAWAKE
PUZZLE 1

WPC 2015 R2 Q15

HEYAWAKE
PUZZLE 2

WPC 2016 R2 Q8

Instructions on page 58

HEYAWAKE
PUZZLE 3

WPC 2017 R12 Q8

HEYAWAKE
PUZZLE 4

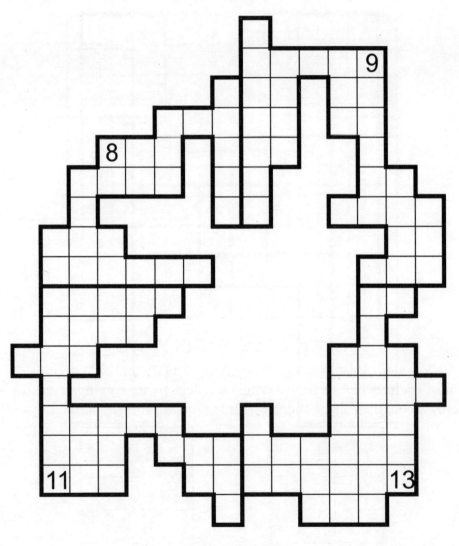

WPC 2011 R5 Q9

Instructions on page 58

HEYAWAKE
SYMMETRY

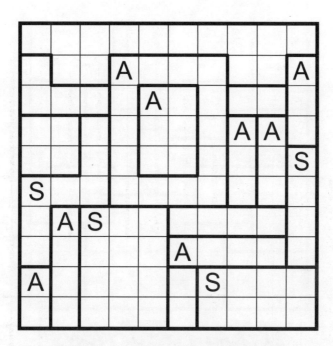

EXTRA INSTRUCTIONS

All 'S' regions must have 180° rotational symmetry, and all 'A' regions must *not* have 180° rotational symmetry. Regions are symmetric if and only if both their shape and their shaded squares are symmetric.

WPC 2013 R5 Q17

HEYAWAKE
AKICHIWAKE

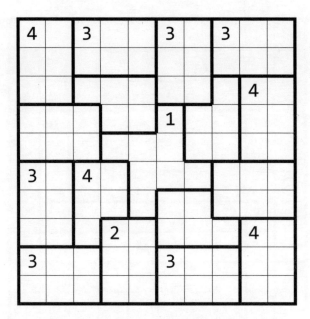

EXTRA INSTRUCTIONS

Numbers now indicate the maximum possible size of the continuous white area within a region. There need not be an area equal to this size, but there can be no continuous area larger than this value.

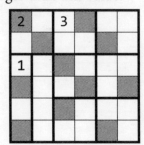

WPC 2017 R4 Q1

Instructions on page 58

6.

HITORI

INSTRUCTIONS

Shade some squares so that no unshaded number repeats within any row or column. Shaded squares cannot touch on any side.

All unshaded squares must form a single connected region. Squares are considered connected if they share a side and are both unshaded.

Example

6	6	3	2	1	5
1	2	6	3	5	4
5	1	4	2	3	4
3	3	3	5	2	1
4	2	1	6	5	3
6	1	5	4	4	4

Solution

6	6	3	2	1	5
1	2	6	3	5	4
5	1	4	2	3	4
3	3	3	5	2	1
4	2	1	6	5	3
6	1	5	4	4	4

WPC 2010 R2 Q5(1)

PUZZLE 1

5	7	2	1	8	5	3	10	5	9
9	3	7	6	10	8	5	4	2	6
7	1	10	4	8	6	7	7	5	10
1	3	4	9	7	8	3	5	8	10
7	2	6	8	6	3	10	1	4	5
8	3	3	5	9	5	6	5	7	5
1	8	1	10	6	9	4	6	1	7
3	10	1	5	6	4	1	9	6	2
4	5	10	7	3	8	1	8	9	4
10	10	8	7	1	2	1	3	6	4

WPC 2010 R2 Q5(2)

HITORI
PUZZLE 2

6	6	9	7	3	1	8	1	3	6
2	3	7	6	9	7	1	8	4	1
5	4	2	3	4	6	9	5	8	5
7	8	4	4	2	10	10	9	10	6
6	10	7	8	9	4	7	10	9	3
8	9	8	5	7	8	1	5	10	4
4	10	3	9	4	5	7	1	9	8
8	2	4	8	3	6	6	4	1	5
5	9	8	2	4	10	3	6	10	9
4	7	5	6	8	7	4	3	6	3

WPC 2015 R2 Q8

Instructions on page 66

PUZZLE 3

6	2	8	9	4	6	8	6	4	10
1	5	6	10	3	4	2	9	2	8
3	4	1	8	1	3	1	10	5	7
5	9	10	4	9	6	2	5	4	10
4	6	8	1	10	9	1	7	3	2
3	9	6	2	8	4	4	1	6	3
6	5	1	5	4	8	1	2	5	4
3	8	2	10	1	7	6	5	10	3
10	7	10	3	8	1	9	7	8	10
8	6	4	6	5	2	4	3	7	9

WPC 2015 R2 Q9

6	10	5	5	11	3	10	4	10	1	2	8
8	6	1	9	10	5	7	2	11	4	8	3
4	9	7	12	6	2	9	3	8	12	7	4
11	5	12	1	4	9	5	11	6	7	3	2
3	11	6	2	5	1	3	5	10	8	12	4
7	1	10	11	2	7	3	6	9	2	5	11
12	7	11	4	9	10	1	9	12	6	5	11
5	4	6	1	3	12	2	12	7	7	11	10
4	5	12	10	6	8	9	8	2	11	6	1
2	3	9	7	12	5	6	1	3	3	4	7
4	8	3	5	5	11	6	2	1	10	8	6
10	1	2	3	7	6	11	10	4	1	9	5

WPC 2012 R5 Q4

Instructions on page 66

STRONG

1	1	4	3	4	1	3	2	2
1	1	2	3	2	1	3	2	2
3	2	1	4	3	3	2	1	3
4	3	4	2	3	1	1	2	4
4	2	1	1	2	3	3	4	1
2	2	3	3	4	4	4	1	2
2	3	3	1	3	2	2	4	1
4	4	2	1	3	1	2	3	3
4	4	2	1	1	1	2	3	3

NEW INSTRUCTIONS

Shaded squares may now touch. Every row and every column must contain at least one unshaded square.

4	2	4	8
8	6	6	8
4	2	6	6
2	2	6	6

4	2	4	8
8	6	6	8
4	2	6	6
2	2	6	6

WPC 2017 R4 Q12

HITORI
REGIONAL 1

	1	2	3	5	4	7
1		3	9	7	2	4
2	4		1	3	9	5
3	8	4		6	1	2
4	5	8	2		7	1
7	6	5	4	2		3
6	2	9	5	1	3	

EXTRA INSTRUCTIONS

Every bold-lined region must also contain distinct digits.

2	2	3	6	4	7
1	5	2	5	3	6
3	1	4	5	7	2
2	3	6	7	1	5
5	4	7	2	6	4
3	4	6	3	7	7

2	2	3	6	4	7
1	5	2	5	3	6
3	1	4	5	7	2
2	3	6	7	1	5
5	4	7	2	6	4
3	4	6	3	7	7

WPC 2017 R4 Q7

Instructions on page 66

HITORI
REGIONAL 2

3	9	6	2	5	1	6	8	7
6	1	2	7	3	3	4	9	5
7	3	9	8	6	9	7	2	5
3	7	5	1	8	4	2	7	8
9	8	8	6	7	4	5	1	4
1	5	9	3	5	8	1	6	4
5	4	1	2	2	6	8	7	9
2	2	3	5	4	3	6	5	1
4	6	8	7	1	9	7	3	2

EXTRA INSTRUCTIONS

Every bold-lined region must also contain distinct digits.

2	2	3	6	4	7
1	5	2	5	3	6
3	1	4	5	7	2
2	3	6	7	1	5
5	4	7	2	6	4
3	4	6	3	7	7

2	2	3	6	4	7
1	5	2	5	3	6
3	1	4	5	7	2
2	3	6	7	1	5
5	4	7	2	6	4
3	4	6	3	7	7

WPC 2017 R4 Q8

HITORI
LETTERS

K	O	P	R	I	V	N	I	C	A
R	L	O	D	S	M	P	T	M	I
Y	P	J	U	L	V	P	E	K	W
D	M	I	A	B	B	J	Z	D	M
G	O	D	R	X	G	L	M	B	S
K	S	E	U	F	I	B	S	W	F
M	Q	A	V	R	B	T	Z	Q	S
N	I	V	H	B	A	I	K	N	H
V	L	D	S	M	J	K	F	B	J
W	P	C	C	R	O	A	T	I	A

EXTRA INSTRUCTIONS

Apply Hitori rules, except with letters instead of with digits. The bold letters have no special meaning – they are for decorative purposes only.

WPC 2016 R12 Q6

Instructions on page 66

7.

KAKURO

Place a digit from 1 to 9 into each white square. Each horizontal run of white squares adds up to the total given at the left of the run, and each vertical run of white squares adds up to the total given at the top of the run. No digit can be used more than once within any run.

Example   **Solution**

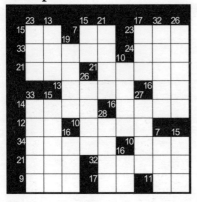

WPC 2013 R2 Q7(1)

KAKURO
PUZZLE 1

WPC 2013 R2 Q7(2)

KAKURO
PUZZLE 2

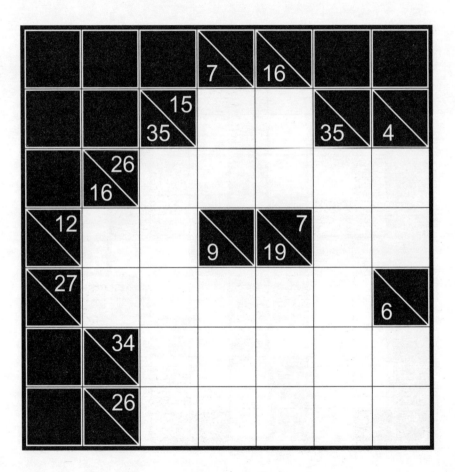

WPC 2010 R2 Q6(1)

Instructions on page 76

KAKURO

PUZZLE 3

WPC 2010 R2 Q6(2)

KAKURO
HEXAKURO 1

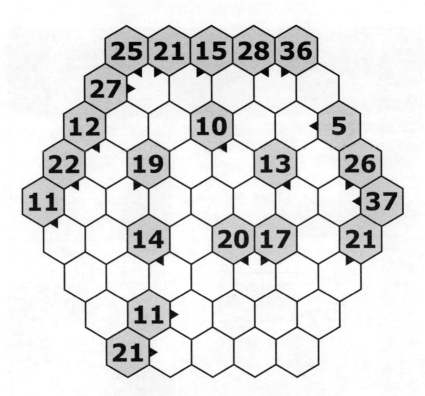

EXTRA INSTRUCTIONS

As per regular kakuro, but rows and columns now run in one of three directions as indicated by the triangular arrows.

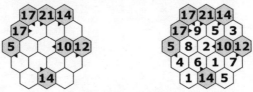

WPC 2008 R2 Q16

Instructions on page 76

KAKURO
HEXAKURO 2

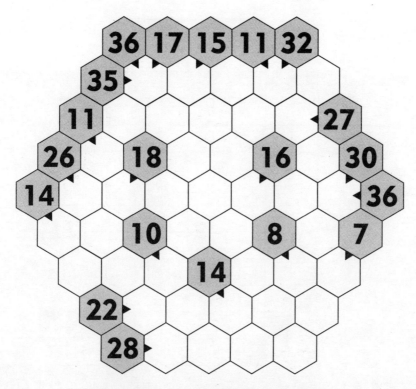

EXTRA INSTRUCTIONS

As per regular kakuro, but rows and columns now run in one of three directions as indicated by the triangular arrows.

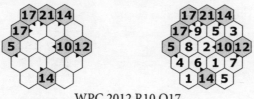

WPC 2012 R10 Q17

KAKURO
SKYKURO

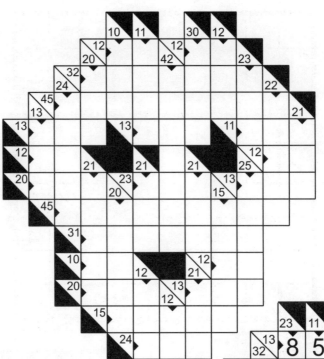

EXTRA RULES

Normal rules apply, but also consider each digit you place to be a building of that many storeys. As well as their usual meaning, one of the two digits in each given clue total reveals the number of buildings visible from that clue. Higher buildings hide lower ones.

WPC 2010 R3 Q6

Instructions on page 76

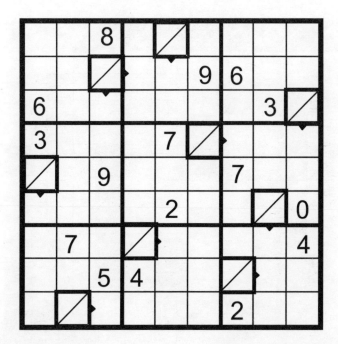

EXTRA RULES

Place 0-9 in each row, column and bold-lined 3×3 box. In squares with diagonal lines, write two digits – one above and one below the line, so that together they form a two-digit number that equals the sum of the digits pointed to by every arrow from that square (i.e. they form a kakuro clue). The sum cannot be a two-digit number that starts with '0'.

WPC 2010 R3 Q7

KAKURO
GAPPED

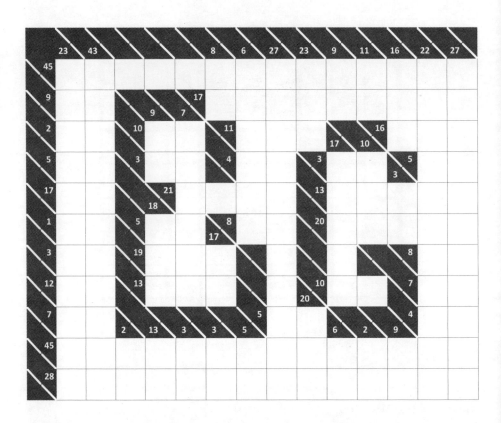

EXTRA INSTRUCTIONS

Some white squares can remain empty. Empty white squares cannot touch, except diagonally.

WPC 2015 R12 Q10

Instructions on page 76

8.

KROPKI

KROPKI INSTRUCTIONS

Place the digits 1-8 (or 1-6 in the example and the puzzles on pages 92 and 93) once each into every row and column.

Squares separated by a white dot must contain digits whose values differ by exactly one. Squares separated by a black dot must contain digits where one square is twice the value of the other. Squares that contain the digits 1 and 2 can be separated by either a black dot *or* a white dot.

All possible dots are shown, so squares *not* separated by dots neither contain consecutive values nor have one value equal to twice the other.

Example

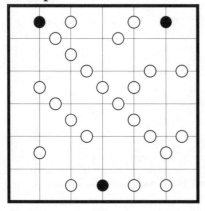

Solution

4	2	1	5	6	3
1	3	4	6	2	5
6	5	3	2	1	4
2	6	5	3	4	1
5	4	6	1	3	2
3	1	2	4	5	6

WPC 2016 R3 Q1

KROPKI
PUZZLE 1

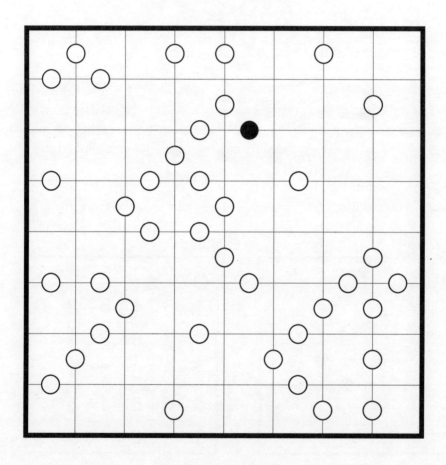

WPC 2016 R3 Q2

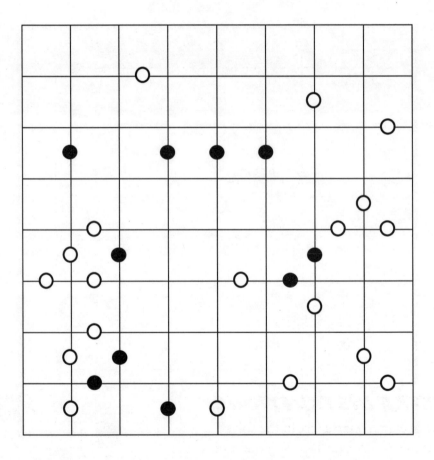

WPC 2014 R4 Q11

Instructions on page 86

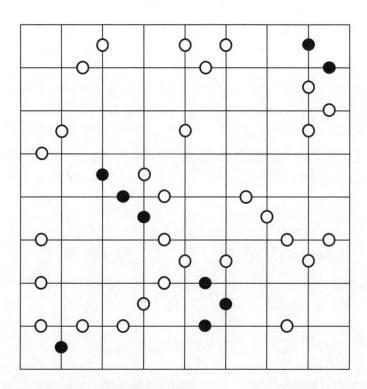

EXTRA INSTRUCTIONS

Shade eight squares (six in the solved example to the right), each containing a different number. These shaded squares will *not* contain any dots between them and their neighbouring squares, whether or not a dot is required by the rules of kropki.

3	5	1	6	2	4
1	2	4	5	6	3
6	3	2	1	4	5
4	1	5	2	3	6
2	4	6	3	5	1
5	6	3	4	1	2

WPC 2014 R4 Q12

KROPKI
HEXA 1

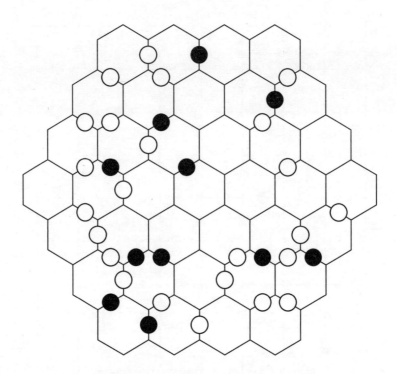

EXTRA INSTRUCTIONS

Rows and columns now run in three directions, and not all rows/columns contain every digit. Place digits from 1 to 7 (1 to 3 in the example), without repeating any digit within a row or column.

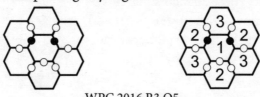

WPC 2016 R3 Q5

Instructions on page 86

KROPKI
HEXA 2

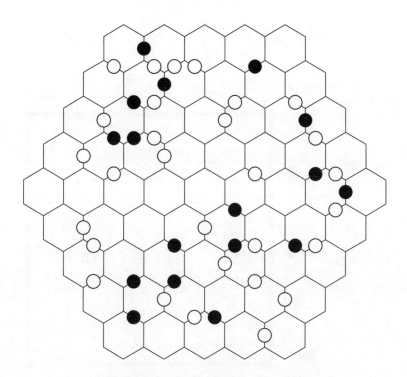

EXTRA INSTRUCTIONS

Rows and columns now run in three directions, and not all rows/columns contain every digit. Place digits from 1 to 9 (1 to 3 in the example), without repeating any digit within a row or column.

WPC 2016 R3 Q6

KROPKI
OUTSIDE 1

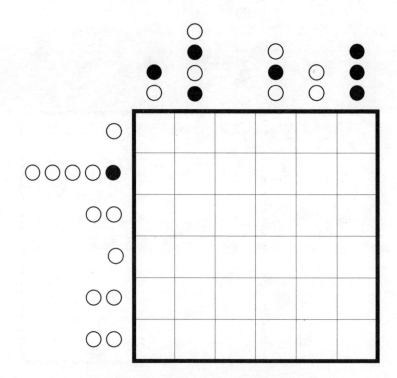

EXTRA INSTRUCTIONS

All dots from every row and column have been removed from the grid and placed outside. They must be placed into their corresponding row or column in the given order, although there may be gaps between the dots.

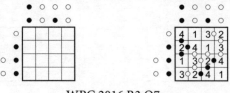

WPC 2016 R3 Q7

Instructions on page 86

KROPKI
OUTSIDE 2

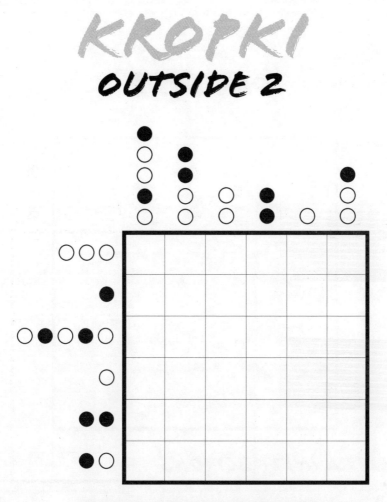

EXTRA INSTRUCTIONS

All dots from every row and column have been removed from the grid and placed outside. They must be placed into their corresponding row or column in the given order, although there may be gaps between the dots.

WPC 2016 R3 Q8

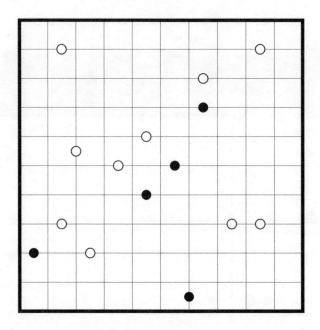

EXTRA INSTRUCTIONS

Draw a single loop that travels horizontally and vertically through the centre of every square. The loop cannot touch or cross itself. The loop must pass through all dots, and the dots provide information about the length of the straight line segments on either side of the dot. If there is a white dot on a straight line, then the loop passes through one more square on one side of the dot than on the other before turning; or if there is a black dot then the loop enters twice as many squares on one side of the dot than the other before turning. The example should help clarify these rules. Not all possible dots have been given.

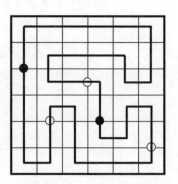

WPC 2016 R3 Q11

Instructions on page 86

KROPKI
LOOP 2

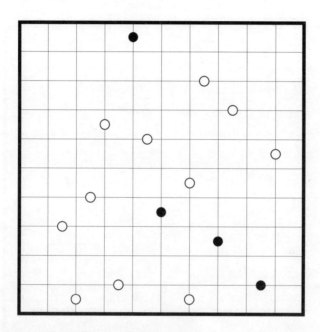

EXTRA INSTRUCTIONS

Draw a single loop that travels horizontally and vertically through the centre of every square. The loop cannot touch or cross itself. The loop must pass through all dots, and the dots provide information about the length of the straight line segments on either side of the dot. If there is a white dot on a straight line, then the loop passes through one more square on one side of the dot than on the other before turning; or if there is a black dot then the loop enters twice as many squares on one side of the dot than the other before turning. The example should help clarify these rules. Not all possible dots have been given.

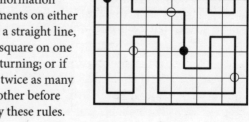

WPC 2016 R3 Q12

KROPKI FILLOMINO

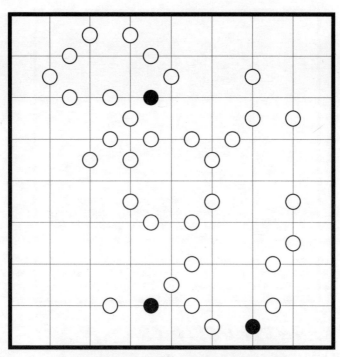

EXTRA INSTRUCTIONS

Divide the grid along the given lines into regions so that no two regions with the same area share a side. Each square must contain a value equal to the size of the region it is in, measured in squares.

WPC 2016 R3 Q13

Instructions on page 86

9.
LITS

LITS

INSTRUCTIONS

Shade some squares so that a single tetromino is formed within each bold-lined area. Tetrominoes must be L, I, T or S shapes, and not a solid 2×2 box – these four options are shown here:

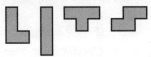

All shaded squares in the puzzle must be connected orthogonally (i.e. touch left/right/up/down), and there may not be any 2×2 areas of squares consisting entirely of shaded squares.

No two of the same type of tetromino (L, I, T or S) may touch along any side. Reflections and rotations of the same type of tetromino still count as the same tetromino, and therefore may not touch.

Example

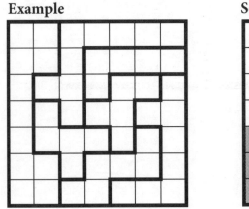

Solution

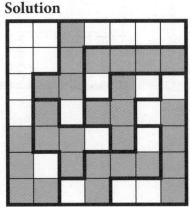

WPC 2011 R14 Q11

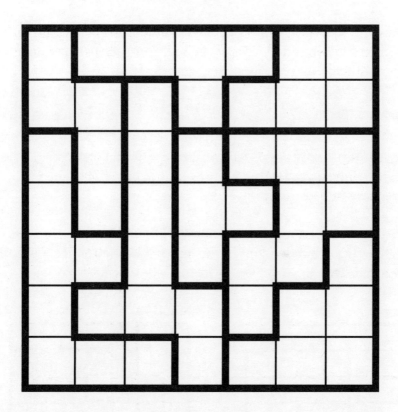

WPC 2011 R2 Q5(1)

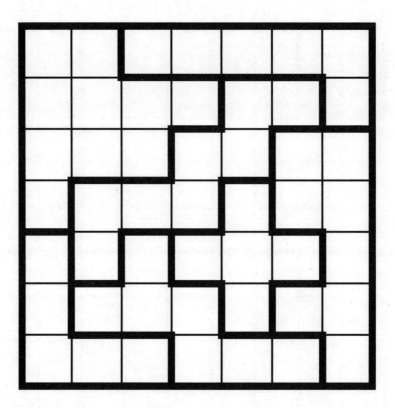

WPC 2011 R2 Q5(2)

Instructions on page 98

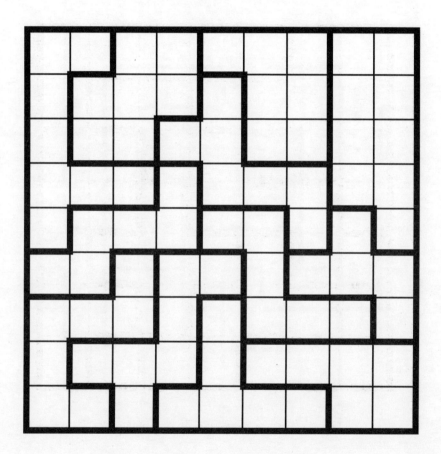

WPC 2011 R2 Q5(3)

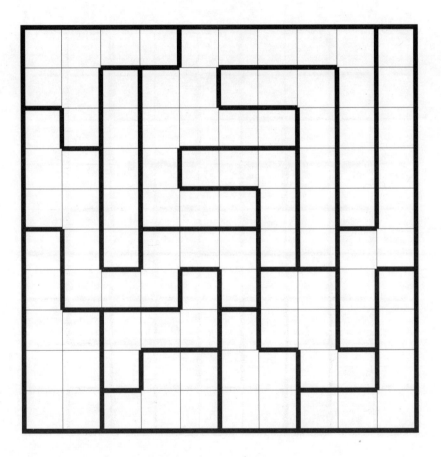

WPC 2016 R2 Q17

Instructions on page 98

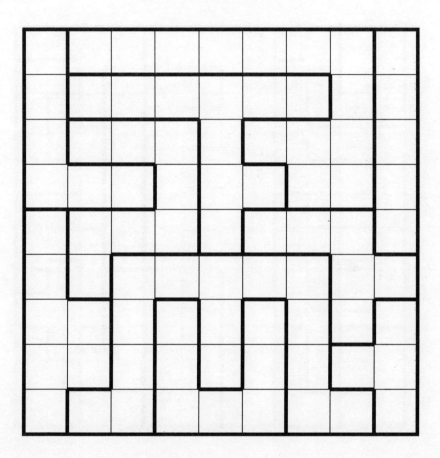

WPC 2017 R1 Q4

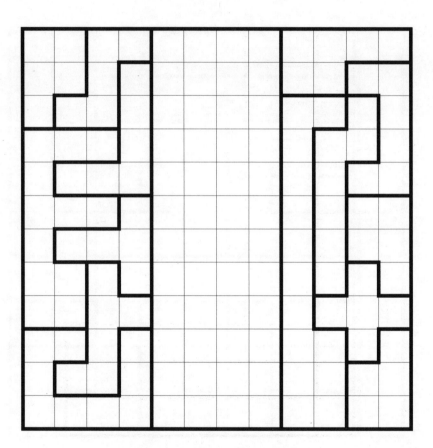

EXTRA INSTRUCTIONS

Standard instructions apply – the large empty area in the middle is simply an unusually large region.

WPC 2016 R9 Q24

Instructions on page 98

PUZZLE 7

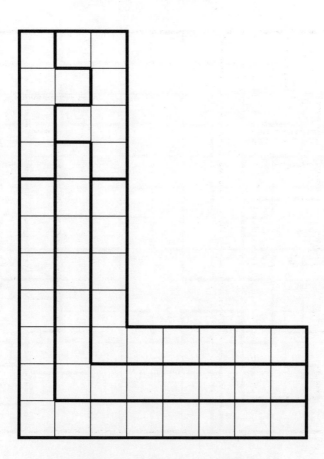

EXTRA INSTRUCTIONS

Standard instructions apply – the unusual L-shaped grid does not change the rules.

WPC 2017 R12 Q12

LITS

DRAGON LITSO

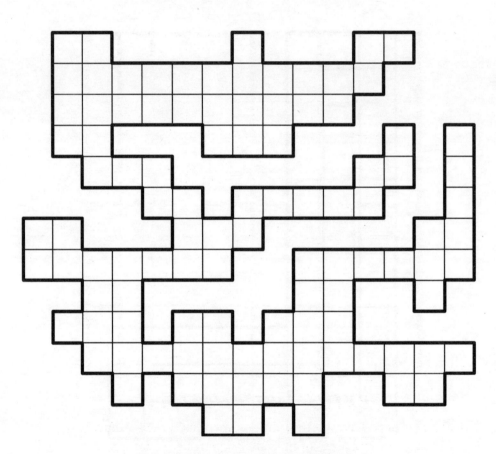

EXTRA INSTRUCTIONS

Divide the grid into tetrominos so that no two identical tetrominos ever share a side. All squares must be part of one tetromino. A 2×2 'O' tetromino *is* allowed, so the set of tetrominos is as shown here:

WPC 2013 R12 Q5

Instructions on page 98

LITS+

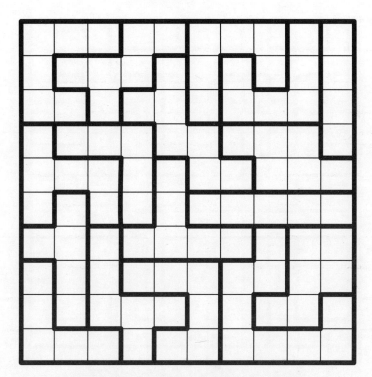

EXTRA INSTRUCTIONS

Not all areas need have a tetromino – some may remain empty.
Additionally, no 2×2 areas of unshaded squares are allowed.

WPC 2014 R11 Q16

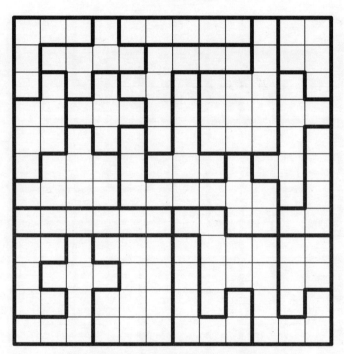

EXTRA INSTRUCTIONS

Form tetrominoes using *unshaded* squares <u>instead of</u> shaded squares, so no two matching tetrominoes share a side. Unlike normal LITS, 2×2 tetrominoes *are* permitted, but *shaded* squares still cannot form 2×2 areas. Identical tetrominoes cannot touch.

WPC 2014 R10 Q5

10.
MASYU

MASYU
INSTRUCTIONS

Draw a single loop, using only horizontal and vertical lines, that travels between the centres of some squares in such a way that the loop does not visit any square more than once.

At every square containing a white circle the loop must pass straight through that circle and make a 90 degree turn in at least one of the squares adjacent to the circle.

At every square containing a black circle the loop must make a 90 degree turn and travel straight through both squares adjacent to the circle.

Example   **Solution**

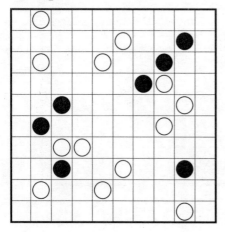
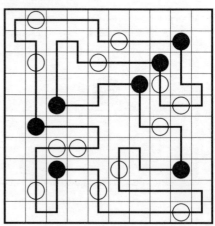

WPC 2017 R3 Q6

MASYU
PUZZLE 1

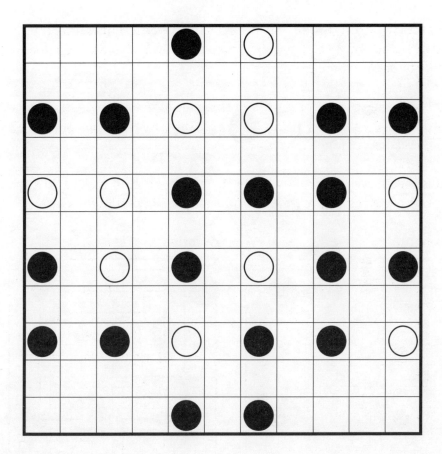

WPC 2017 R3 Q5

MASYU
PUZZLE 2

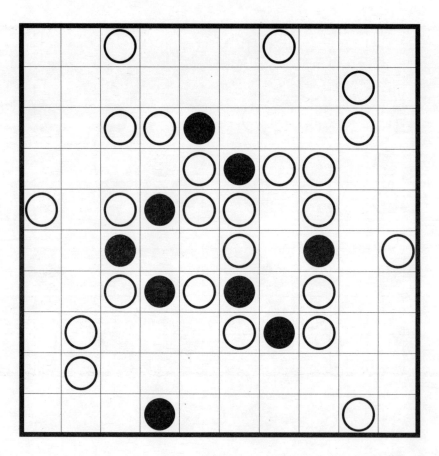

WPC 2016 R2 Q20

Instructions on page 110

MASYU
PUZZLE 3

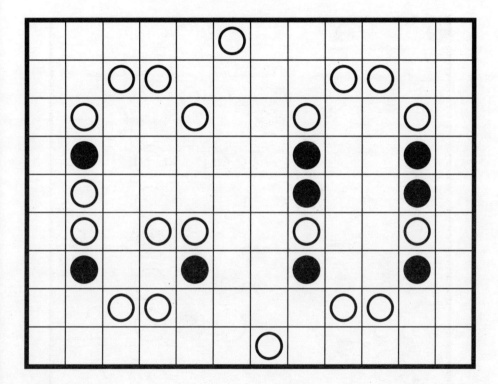

WPC 2013 R7 Q4

MASYU
PUZZLE 4

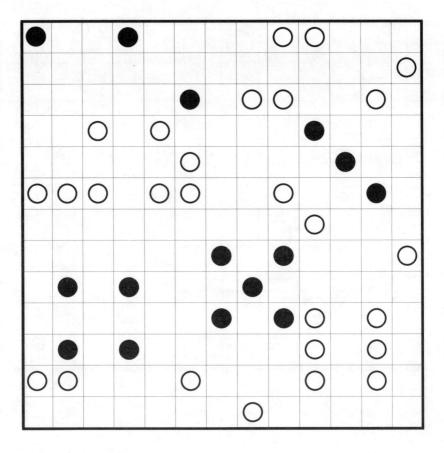

WPC 2015 R11 Q12

Instructions on page 110

MASYU
PUZZLE 5

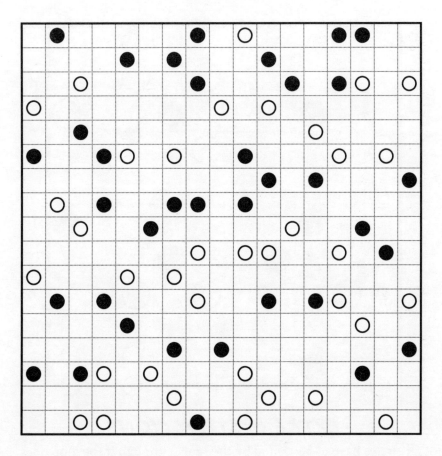

WPC 2014 R3 Q27

MASYU
REVERSE

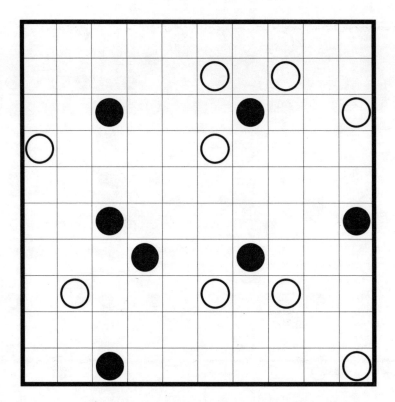

EXTRA INSTRUCTIONS

Not all circles have to be visited by the loop, although if the loop *does* visit them then normal Masyu rules apply. However, all *blank* squares *must* be visited by the loop.

WPC 2016 R11 Q14

Instructions on page 110

MASYU REVERSE

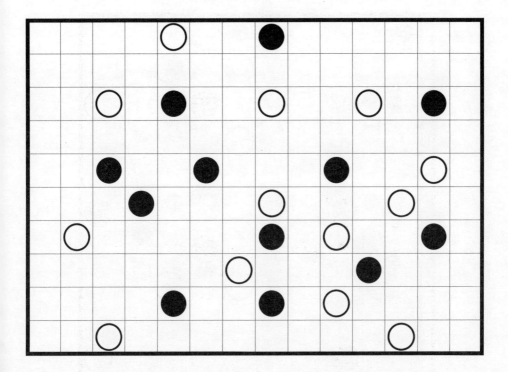

EXTRA INSTRUCTIONS

Not all circles have to be visited by the loop, although if the loop *does* visit them then normal Masyu rules apply. However, all *blank* squares *must* be visited by the loop.

WPC 2016 R11 Q15

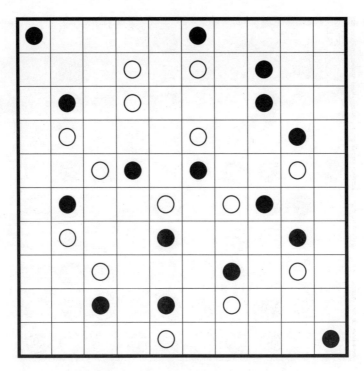

EXTRA INSTRUCTIONS

The loop must make a turn in the squares immediately before and after each white circle, and go straight through at least one of the squares immediately before or after each black circle.

WPC 2017 R4 Q2

Instructions on page 110

MASYU
FULL

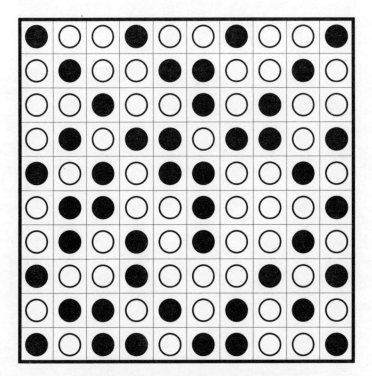

EXTRA INSTRUCTIONS

Find a valid Masyu solution. Not all circles need be used.

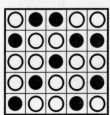
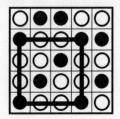

WPC 2016 R4 Q6

MASYU
HEXAGONAL

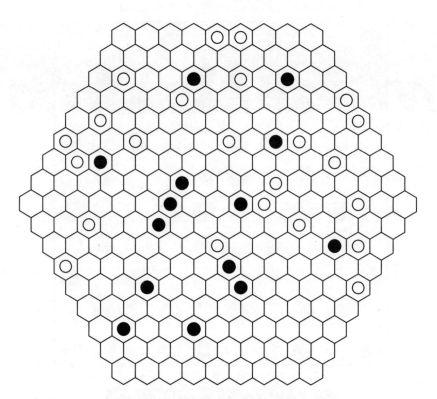

EXTRA INSTRUCTIONS

Join hexagons using lines between the centres of hexagons that share a side. Otherwise, normal rules apply.

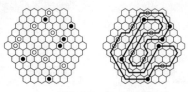

WPC 2010 R9 Q9

Instructions on page 110

11.
NUMBER LINK

NUMBER LINK
INSTRUCTIONS

Draw a series of separate paths, each connecting a pair of identical numbers or letters. No more than one line can enter any square, and lines can only travel horizontally or vertically between the centres of squares.

Example

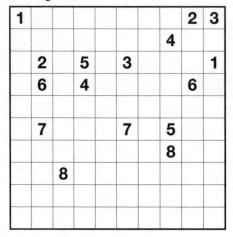

Solution

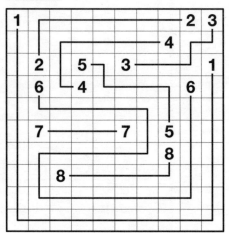

WPC 2014 R6 Q1

NUMBER LINK

PUZZLE 1

WPC 2013 R7 Q2

NUMBER LINK
PUZZLE 2

WPC 2017 R16 Q10

Instructions on page 122

NUMBER LINK

PUZZLE 3

WPC 2009 R2 Q1

NUMBER LINK

PUZZLE 4

WPC 2012 R7 Q14

Instructions on page 122

NUMBER LINK
PUZZLE 5

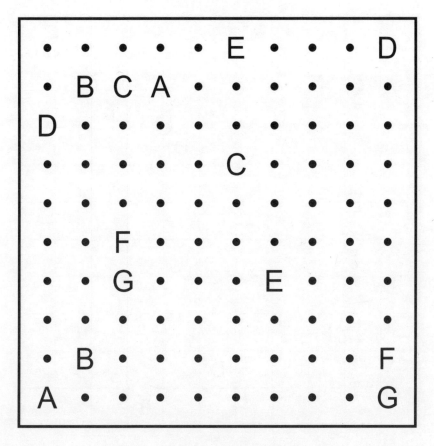

EXTRA INSTRUCTIONS

This puzzle solves in the same way as the previous ones, except that square centres are marked with dots and the squares themselves are not shown.

WPC 2008 R2 Q17(1)

NUMBER LINK
PUZZLE 6

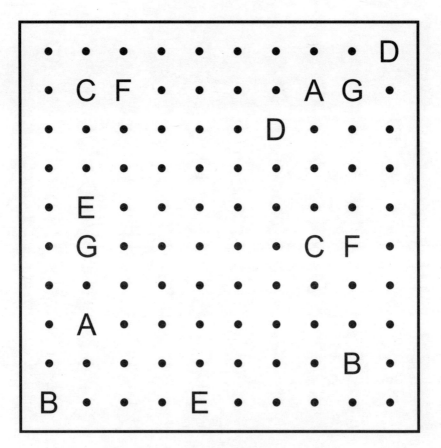

EXTRA INSTRUCTIONS

This puzzle solves in the same way as the previous ones, except that square centres are marked with dots and the squares themselves are not shown.

WPC 2008 R2 Q17(2)

Instructions on page 122

NUMBER LINK
NO 2x2

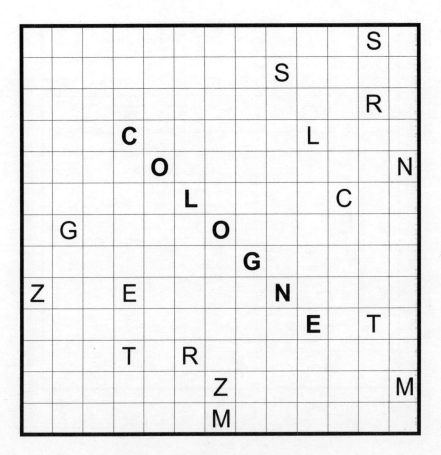

EXTRA INSTRUCTIONS

A single path cannot visit all 4 squares in any 2×2 area. (The bold letters are for decorative purposes only, and do not affect the solution).

WPC 2016 R12 Q3

NUMBER LINK
MISSING LETTERS

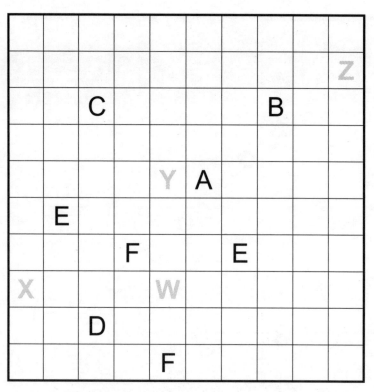

W ☐ ≠ X ☐ ≠ Y ☐ ≠ Z ☐

EXTRA INSTRUCTIONS

W, X, Y and Z must be replaced with A, B, C or D in order to create a regular number link puzzle.

WPC 2012 R13 Q13

Instructions on page 122

NUMBERLINK
TOROIDAL

			1		**2**		
3	**4**						
	5			**6**			
				7	**4**	**8**	
2			**1**				
			5		**8**		
7							
	3		**6**				

EXTRA INSTRUCTIONS

Paths can travel off one end of a row or column and re-enter at the opposite end of the same row or column, respectively.

WPC 2014 R12 Q9

NUMBER LINK
DIAGONAL

1	2	3	4		3
			5		
	4				
	1			6	
6	2				5

EXTRA INSTRUCTIONS

Paths can also travel diagonally between squares. They may cross on the junction between four squares.

 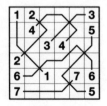

WPC 2014 R11 Q3

Instructions on page 122

12.
NURIKABE

NUKIKABE
INSTRUCTIONS

Shade some squares so that every number in the puzzle remains as part of a continuous unshaded area of precisely the given number of squares. There must be exactly one number per unshaded area.

Shaded squares cannot form any 2×2 areas, and all shaded squares must form one continuous area. Squares are considered continuous if they share a side.

Example

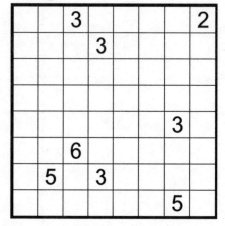

Solution

WPC 2013 R2 Q1(1)

NURIKABE
PUZZLE 1

				5						
								4		
						4				7
			2			1		3		
				2						
8					1					
		8		2					3	
							2			
	3				8					
1										

WPC 2013 R2 Q1(2)

NURIKABE
PUZZLE 2

			2					
	5			6				
		8				2		
5			2					
	3				5			
		5						

WPC 2016 R9 Q27

Instructions on page 134

NURIKABE
PUZZLE 3

1			2			4			2
2			3			3			1
2			7			6			2
3			3			2			4

WPC 2016 R9 Q28

NURIKABE
PUZZLE 4

6							
		2		4			3
	3			3			
						2	
		4					
			3				
	2						2

WPC 2015 R11 Q18

Instructions on page 134

NURIKABE
PUZZLE 5

							6	
	2		6			18		
								5
5								
	2			1		5		
	3							

WPC 2013 R6 Q15

NURIKABE
PUZZLE 6

WPC 2016 R2 Q6

Instructions on page 134

NURIKABE
PUZZLE 7

26			20			17			2			2			1
5			7			5			8			1			7
2			2			1			2			3			8
3			1			1			7			2			18
8			1			15			10			1			2
5			1			3			9			5			2

WPC 2017 R9 Q8

Instructions on page 134

NURIKABE
DOUBLED

EXTRA INSTRUCTIONS

Each region now contains exactly two numbers, and must be of a size exactly equal to the sum of those two numbers.

WPC 2013 R6 Q16

Instructions on page 134

NURIKABE
FULL

5	3	3	3	3	6	6	4	4	4	4	2
5	7	7	7	6	6	6	6	4	2	2	2
5	5	7	7	4	4	4	6	4	2	5	5
5	4	7	7	7	7	4	4	2	2	6	5
5	4	4	5	5	5	5	7	7	2	6	5
4	4	4	5	6	6	6	7	6	6	6	5
4	6	4	5	5	6	7	7	7	6	6	5
6	6	6	6	3	6	6	6	7	6	6	4
6	6	6	6	3	3	6	6	7	7	6	4
6	2	2	3	3	4	6	6	7	5	6	4
6	2	2	4	4	4	7	7	7	5	4	4
6	6	7	7	7	7	7	5	5	5	5	4

EXTRA INSTRUCTIONS

Shade some squares so that what remains is a valid Nurikabe solution, except that the same number will repeat in every square of each region.

5	5	5	5	5
3	3	5	1	5
5	5	5	5	5
5	1	1	3	3
5	5	2	2	3

WPC 2016 R4 Q7

NURIKABE
WORD

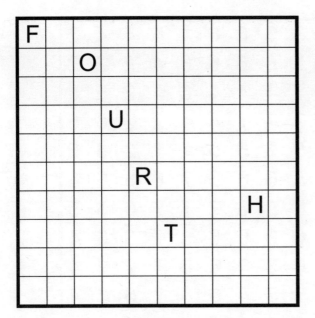

DEFT
DEDUCTION
DONE
DERIVES
DETECTABLE
DELIGHT

EXTRA INSTRUCTIONS

Place every letter of the listed words so that they can be read in the grid by tracing a path from the first to the last letter, moving left/right/up/down between squares. The squares of each word form a single Nurikabe region, instead of a given digit. One letter from each word is given.

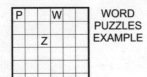

WORD
PUZZLES
EXAMPLE

WPC 2013 R5 Q12

Instructions on page 134

13.
RECTANGLES

RECTANGLES
INSTRUCTIONS

Draw along some of the grid lines in order to divide the grid up into a set of rectangles, such that every number is inside exactly one rectangle.

The number inside each rectangle must be exactly equal to the number of grid squares that the rectangle contains. All grid squares are covered by exactly one rectangle.

Example   **Solution**

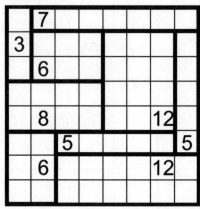

WPC 2011 R9 Q4(1)

RECTANGLES
PUZZLE 1

	2				4		
			9			6	
	3		9				6
5		9					
	6					2	
			6				3
				9			
2							

WPC 2011 R9 Q4(2)

RECTANGLES
PUZZLE 2

WPC 2011 R9 Q4(3)

Instructions on page 146

RECTANGLES
PUZZLE 3

WPC 2011 R9 Q4(4)

RECTANGLES
PUZZLE 4

WPC 2013 R6 Q13

Instructions on page 146

RECTANGLES
PUZZLE 5

		2				5			
			6						
4		6			2				2
			4		6				2
		5						4	
					4		2		
					1				
	6		3					3	
1					2				2

WPC 2015 R12 Q8

RECTANGLES
PUZZLE 6

WPC 2016 R2 Q12

Instructions on page 146

RECTANGLES
PUZZLE 7

							14		
			6		15				
12								5	
		11							12
		12					12		
	10			12					
							10	3	
	3	3			4				

WPC 2008 R2 Q4

RECTANGLES
PUZZLE 8

3			5			6				6		
				3			4			3		2
	6	3		8				10				
					4						8	
	9					4			2	3		
		5	3					8				
4					12					6		
		6								3		5
2				7					4	8		3
	4				8							
	6							6	2			
			4	4			10				7	

WPC 2014 R3 Q24

Instructions on page 146

RECTANGLES
DOUBLED

			8					
		3					4	
	5				3			6
			6			4		
		4						8
9							2	
			4			4		
	3			2				4
		6					8	
				7				

EXTRA INSTRUCTIONS

Each rectangle will contain two numbers, and must have an area equal to the sum of those two numbers.

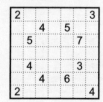

WPC 2013 R6 Q14

RECTANGLES
OVERLAPPING

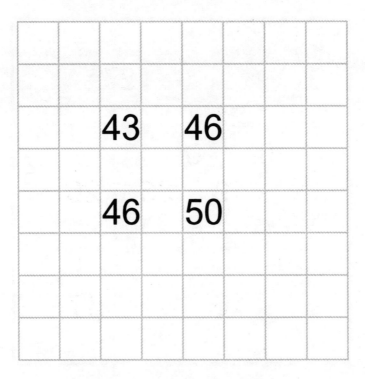

NEW INSTRUCTIONS

Draw rectangles along some of the grid lines so that no two rectangles share a corner or part of any side, and each number indicates the total area of all of the rectangles it is contained in. Rectangles can overlap.

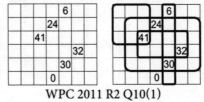

WPC 2011 R2 Q10(1)

Full instructions on this page

RECTANGLES
OVERLAPPING

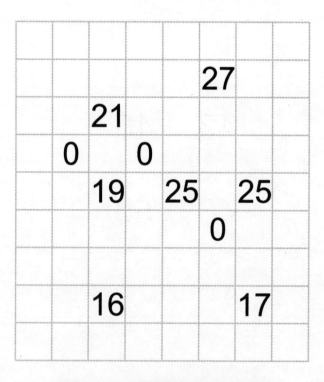

NEW INSTRUCTIONS

Draw rectangles along some of the grid lines so that no two rectangles share a corner or part of any side, and each number indicates the total area of all of the rectangles it is contained in. Rectangles can overlap.

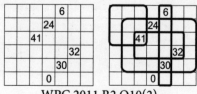

WPC 2011 R2 Q10(2)

RECTANGLES
CODED

	2	6					
I							
	N						
	D				W		
		I					
		A			P		
					C		

EXTRA INSTRUCTIONS

Some numbers have been replaced by letters. Same letters represent the same value. Different letters represent different values to other letters (but a letter is permitted to match the value of a given numeric clue). Letters can only take on values from 1 to 10.

WPC 2017 R1 Q10

Instructions on page 146

14.
SLITHERLINK

SLITHERLINK
INSTRUCTIONS

Draw a single loop by connecting together some dots so that each numbered square has the specified number of adjacent line segments.

Dots can only be joined by straight horizontal or vertical lines, and the loop cannot touch, cross or overlap itself in any way.

Example   **Solution**

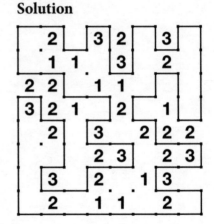

SLITHERLINK
PUZZLE 1

```
.   .   .   .   .   .   .   .   .   .
   2   0   2       2   2   3
.   .   .   .   .   .   .   .   .   .
       2       1       2       3
.   .   .   .   .   .   .   .   .   .
       3   3           1       2
.   .   .   .   .   .   .   .   .   .
 2   2               3
.   .   .   .   .   .   .   .   .   .
 1               2
.   .   .   .   .   .   .   .   .   .
           2                       3
.   .   .   .   .   .   .   .   .   .
       3                   2   2
.   .   .   .   .   .   .   .   .   .
 2       0           1       3
.   .   .   .   .   .   .   .   .   .
 2       2       2       3
.   .   .   .   .   .   .   .   .   .
   1   0   1       1   1   2
.   .   .   .   .   .   .   .   .   .
```

WPC 2013 R2 Q2(1)

SLITHERLINK
PUZZLE 2

```
·   ·   ·   ·   ·   ·   ·   ·   ·   ·
  3   1       2       1           3
·   ·   ·   ·   ·   ·   ·   ·   ·   ·
              2   3           2       3
·   ·   ·   ·   ·   ·   ·   ·   ·   ·
              2
·   ·   ·   ·   ·   ·   ·   ·   ·   ·
  2       2   3       2   3   3       1
·   ·   ·   ·   ·   ·   ·   ·   ·   ·
                  3       2
·   ·   ·   ·   ·   ·   ·   ·   ·   ·
          2       1   1   1   2
·   ·   ·   ·   ·   ·   ·   ·   ·   ·
  2   1   2                       3
·   ·   ·   ·   ·   ·   ·   ·   ·   ·
  2           3   1           1   1   3
·   ·   ·   ·   ·   ·   ·   ·   ·   ·
  2           3   1   3
·   ·   ·   ·   ·   ·   ·   ·   ·   ·
              2           1       1
·   ·   ·   ·   ·   ·   ·   ·   ·   ·
```

WPC 2015 R2 Q18

Instructions on page 160

SLITHERLINK
PUZZLE 3

```
.   .   .   .   .   .   .   .   .   .   .   .   .
   2       3       3   3       3       2       3
.   .   .   .   .   .   .   .   .   .   .   .   .
   1   2       2       0           3       3
.   .   .   .   .   .   .   .   .   .   .   .   .
 3     3           3       1   2   1   2
.   .   .   .   .   .   .   .   .   .   .   .   .
 2     2       3   2           3       2
.   .   .   .   .   .   .   .   .   .   .   .   .
   3   2       2       2       1   2
.   .   .   .   .   .   .   .   .   .   .   .   .
   1       0           1   3       3       2
.   .   .   .   .   .   .   .   .   .   .   .   .
   2   3   2   3       3           3       2
.   .   .   .   .   .   .   .   .   .   .   .   .
   2       2           2       2       2   2
.   .   .   .   .   .   .   .   .   .   .   .   .
 3     3       2       2   3       3       3
.   .   .   .   .   .   .   .   .   .   .   .   .
```

WPC 2014 R3 Q1

SLITHERLINK
PUZZLE 4

```
.   .   .   .   .   .   .   .   .   .   .
      3     1     3     3  3
.   .   .   .   .   .   .   .   .   .   .
  1     1           1     1           3
.   .   .   .   .   .   .   .   .   .   .
    3           3                 1
.   .   .   .   .   .   .   .   .   .   .
    2         0  1     2  2  2        2
.   .   .   .   .   .   .   .   .   .   .
  2  1     2  1  1     2              1
.   .   .   .   .   .   .   .   .   .   .
  2                 2  2     2  1
.   .   .   .   .   .   .   .   .   .   .
  2  1  1  1  2  2     2           1
.   .   .   .   .   .   .   .   .   .   .
       0     2        3     1     2
.   .   .   .   .   .   .   .   .   .   .
    2  1        1  2  1        2  2  3
.   .   .   .   .   .   .   .   .   .   .
      2  0  2     1        3
.   .   .   .   .   .   .   .   .   .   .
    1        2  3        3     3  2  2
.   .   .   .   .   .   .   .   .   .   .
       3     3           2        3  2
.   .   .   .   .   .   .   .   .   .   .
    2  2  1        2        1  2
.   .   .   .   .   .   .   .   .   .   .
  2  2           3              2  3
.   .   .   .   .   .   .   .   .   .   .
```

WPC 2015 R2 Q18

Instructions on page 160

SLITHERLINK
PUZZLE 5

```
    2  2  3     1  3              1  2  3
  1                 2     3  1         1
  1     2        3              2  3  0
     2  1                               2
  2  1              1  2           2     1
     2              3  3     2
  2     2     1              0  1     3  2
  0  2     3  1              2     2     2
              2     1  2              3
  2     3           3  1              2  3
  2                                3  1
     2  2  2              1        2     2
  2           0  2     0                 1
  1  3  1           2  1     2  2  1
```

WPC 2013 R2 Q2(2)

SLITHERLINK
PUZZLE 6

		3	1					
	3	2			3	0		0
								3
	3		0	0		1		2
	1					1		1
3			3				3	
1			3		2	2	0	
	0							
	2		3	2			0	3
				2	0			

EXTRA INSTRUCTIONS

Although this puzzle is drawn with dotted lines instead of dots on the corners, it solves in exactly the same way.

WPC 2016 R9 Q7

Instructions on page 160

SLITHERLINK
PUZZLE 7

0				1	2				2
	3		3			1		2	
		1					3		
	0		2	1	1	2		3	
1			1			3			2
2			3			1			1
	1		2	2	3	1		2	
		3					2		
	1		1			2		3	
3				1	2				2

EXTRA INSTRUCTIONS

Although this puzzle is drawn with dotted lines instead of dots on the corners, it solves in exactly the same way.

WPC 2016 Q9 Q8

SLITHERLINK
PUZZLE 8

```
3 2 1   1 1 1   2 2 2   1 2 2   3 1 2
1   3   1     1   1   1   1   2   2   1
0 1 2   1 1 1   3 3 2   3 2 2   2 1 2


2 2   1 3   1 2 3   3 2 2   1 2   1 1
2 3   1 2   1 1 1   1 1 2   1 2   1 1


1 2 3   3 2 2   2   1   1 3 2   1 2 2
      1   0       0   2   2   2   0   2
3 2 2   2 1 3   1   2   2 2 2   3
2       3   2   2 3 1   2       1   3
2 1 2   2 2 1   2 2 2   2       2 1 2


1 1   1 1   1 2 2   1 1 3   3 1   2 2
1 1   1 1   1 3 2   3 2 1   3 0   2 1


2 3 2   1 1 2   2 1 2   2 2 1   2 1 3
2   1   1   2   3   1   1   1   1   3
1 2 2   2 2 3   2 1 1   2 3 2   2 3 2
```

WPC 2017 R9 Q7

Instructions on page 160

SLITHERLINK
CODED

EXTRA INSTRUCTIONS

Each digit has been replaced by a letter. All instances of the same letter must become the same number, and different letters must become different numbers.

WPC 2017 R1 Q2

SLITHERLINK
SWITCH

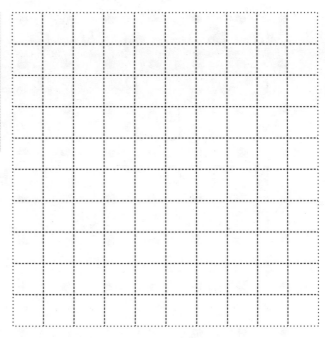

EXTRA INSTRUCTIONS

Copy the small grid onto the empty grid, and solve as normal. However, every clue must switch position with a touching clue left/right/up/down.

WPC 2009 R3 Q4

Instructions on page 160

SLITHERLINK
ODD INNER NUMBERS

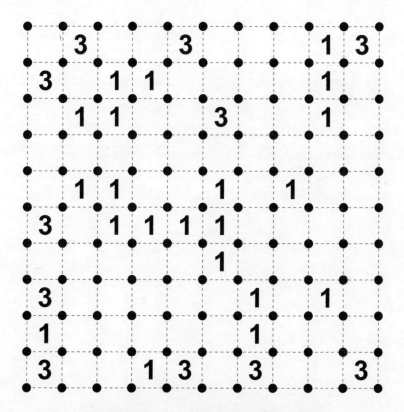

EXTRA INSTRUCTIONS

All possible odd clues *inside the loop* are given.

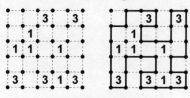

WPC 2009 R8 Q4

SLITHERLINK
EVEN/ODD 1

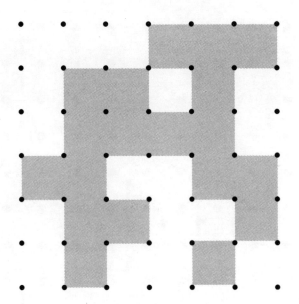

EXTRA INSTRUCTIONS

All grey squares contain a '2' clue, and all white squares contain either a '1' or a '3' clue.

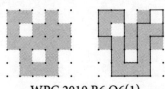

WPC 2010 R6 Q6(1)

Instructions on page 160

SLITHERLINK
EVEN/ODD 2

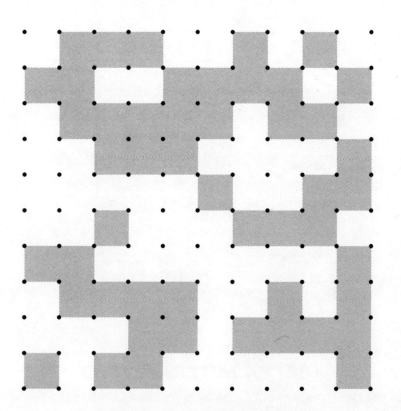

EXTRA INSTRUCTIONS

All grey squares contain a '2' clue, and all white squares contain either a '1' or a '3' clue.

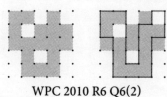

WPC 2010 R6 Q6(2)

SLITHERLINK
OUTSIDE FALSE

```
·   ·   ·   ·   ·   ·   ·   ·   ·   ·   ·   ·
  2   1   3       1   3       1   1   2
·   ·   ·   ·   ·   ·   ·   ·   ·   ·   ·   ·
  3           1   3               1
·   ·   ·   ·   ·   ·   ·   ·   ·   ·   ·   ·
  1   0                       3   3
·   ·   ·   ·   ·   ·   ·   ·   ·   ·   ·   ·
          0           2
·   ·   ·   ·   ·   ·   ·   ·   ·   ·   ·   ·
  1   2       3   3           0   1
·   ·   ·   ·   ·   ·   ·   ·   ·   ·   ·   ·
  2   2       0   2           1   1
·   ·   ·   ·   ·   ·   ·   ·   ·   ·   ·   ·
          2           2
·   ·   ·   ·   ·   ·   ·   ·   ·   ·   ·   ·
  1   0                       0   3
·   ·   ·   ·   ·   ·   ·   ·   ·   ·   ·   ·
  3           2   1               3
·   ·   ·   ·   ·   ·   ·   ·   ·   ·   ·   ·
  2   2   0       1   3       0   3   2
·   ·   ·   ·   ·   ·   ·   ·   ·   ·   ·   ·
```

EXTRA INSTRUCTIONS

Only the clue numbers *inside* the loop are correct. All of the numbers *outside* the loop differ by one from the correct value.

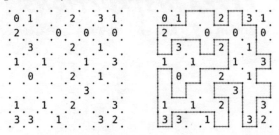

WPC 2014 R9 Q11

Instructions on page 160

15.
TENTS

Attach a tent to each tree, in a horizontally or vertically adjacent square. Squares containing tents cannot touch each other, not even diagonally.

Numbers outside the grid reveal the number of tents in that row or column.

Example   **Solution**

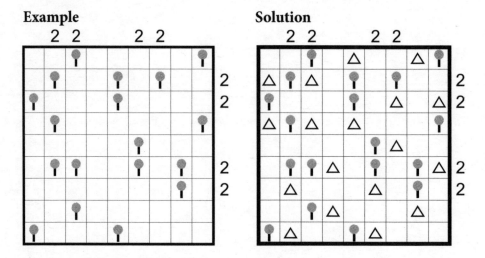

WPC 2016 R2 Q22

TENTS
PUZZLE 1

	3	1	3	2	1	3	1	2	2	1
2				🌳					🌳	
2	🌳						🌳			
2					🌳					
2	🌳									
2					🌳		🌳	🌳	🌳	
3		🌳			🌳					
1										🌳
1			🌳			🌳				
1									🌳	
3		🌳		🌳			🌳			

WPC 2013 R6 Q7

TENTS
PUZZLE 2

	2	3	1	3	1	3	2	2	1
2		🌴						🌴	
3						🌴		🌴	
1	🌴			🌴					
3									🌴
1	🌴		🌴				🌴		
3			🌴				🌴		
2					🌴			🌴	
2				🌴					🌴
1		🌴					🌴		
			🌴			🌴		🌴	

WPC 2017 R3 Q15

Instructions on page 176

TENTS
PUZZLE 3

	3		3		3		3		3	

WPC 2017 R3 Q16

TENTS
PUZZLE 4

```
                                    🌳             2
        🌳                                     🌳  1
                        🌳                         2
  🌳              🌳              🌳                 2
                                🌳                 1
     🌳  🌳              🌳                         2
                                      🌳           2
                 🌳              🌳           🌳     1
        🌳        🌳                                4
                 🌳                                 1

  1  2  1  3  1  2  2  2  1  3
```

WPC 2013 R4 Q2

Instructions on page 176

TENTS
PUZZLE 5

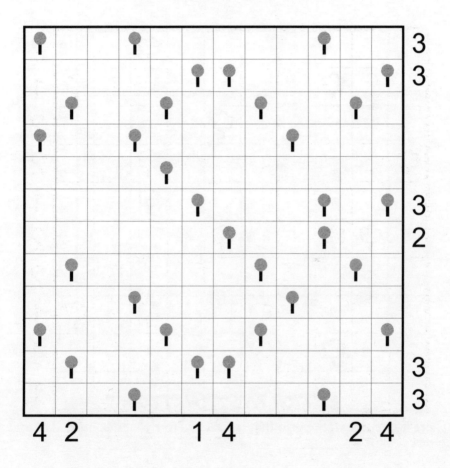

WPC 2016 R16 Q2

TENTS

FRIENDLY CAMPERS 1

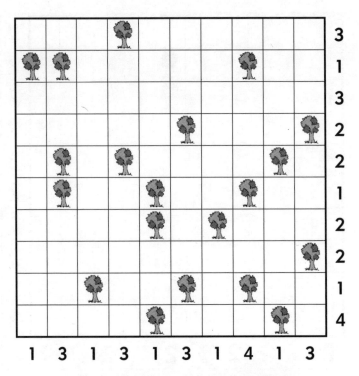

EXTRA INSTRUCTIONS

There is one tree in the grid that is attached to two tents, instead of one.

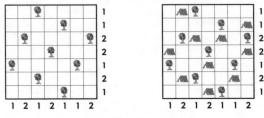

WPC 2012 R3 Q8

Instructions on page 176

FRIENDLY CAMPERS 2

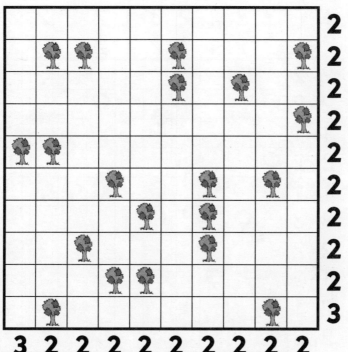

EXTRA INSTRUCTIONS

There is one tree in the grid that is attached to two tents, instead of one.

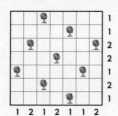 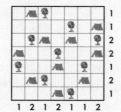

WPC 2012 R14 Q4

TENTS DOUBLED

(puzzle grid — Tents Doubled)

EXTRA INSTRUCTIONS

Each tree has both a black tent and a white tent attached. Tents of the same colour are not allowed to touch, not even diagonally. Tents of different colours can touch, but not overlap. Numbers outside the grid show the number of white or black tents in that row or column.

WPC 2013 Q6 Q8

Instructions on page 176

TENTS
HEXAGONAL

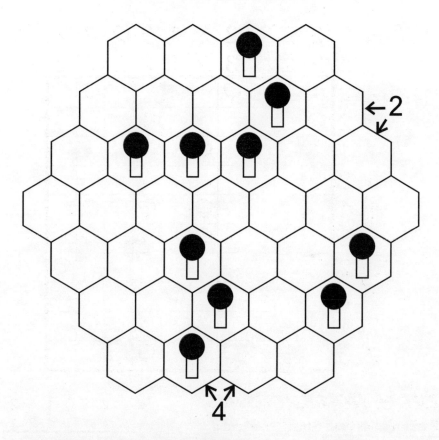

EXTRA INSTRUCTIONS

The grid is now hexagonal, with up to six locations next to each tree. Numbers outside the grid give the *sum* of the number of tents visible in the two directions indicated.

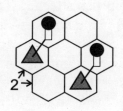

WPC 2011 R13 Q1

TENTS
HEXAGONAL

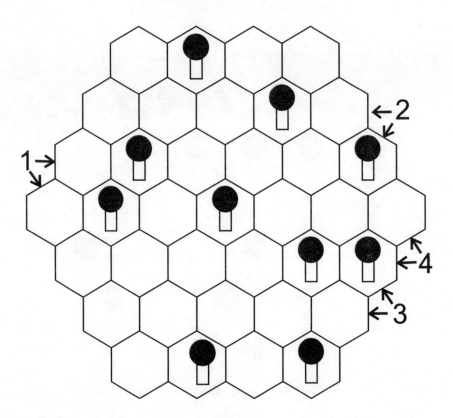

EXTRA INSTRUCTIONS

The grid is now hexagonal, with up to six locations next to each tree. Numbers outside the grid give the *sum* of the number of tents visible in the two directions indicated.

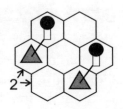

WPC 2011 R13 Q2

Instructions on page 176

16.
YAJILIN

YAJILIN
INSTRUCTIONS

Shade some of the empty squares and draw a single loop which visits every empty unshaded square. The loop can only be drawn with horizontal and vertical lines, and cannot visit any square more than once. Squares with clues in cannot be shaded and must not be visited by the loop.

Numbers with arrows indicate the exact number of shaded squares in a given direction in a specific row or column (all the way from the arrow to the end of that row or column, irrespective of other clues), but not all shaded squares are necessarily pointed at by arrows.

Shaded squares cannot touch on a side, although they may touch diagonally.

Example

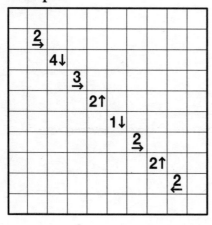

Solution

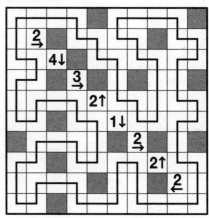

WPC 2014 instruction booklet

YAJILIN
PUZZLE 1

2▶									
		◀0					0▶		
					◀0				
			◀1			0▲			
		◀0				0▶			0▲
				◀0			0▶		
		◀0							
					◀1	1▶			
		◀0					0▶		
					◀0				

WPC 2015 R11 Q24

YAJILIN
PUZZLE 2

WPC 2013 R6 Q1

Instructions on page 188

YAJILIN
PUZZLE 3

								1▾			◂1
1▸			1▾						1▾		
2▾		3▸	2▸								
	1▾		1▾		1▴	2▾	2▸				
				◂2	0▸	0▾					
				0▾				◂0	1▴	1▾	
4▸				◂2			◂3				
				1▸			◂1				
		3▴					0▸				
			0▸					0▴	◂1	1▴	
			◂0								

WPC 2015 R2 Q19

YAJILIN
PUZZLE 4

WPC 2016 R2 Q3

Instructions on page 188

YAJILIN
PUZZLE 5

WPC 2015 R12 Q9

YAJILIN
EXTRA 1

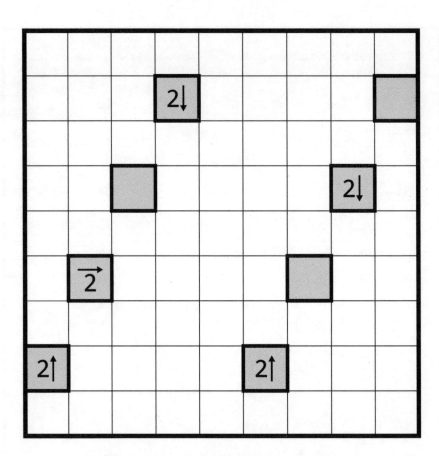

EXTRA INSTRUCTIONS

Some clue squares are empty. Treat them as if they were normal clue squares in terms of solving – i.e. do not count them as shaded squares.

WPC 2017 R3 Q19

Instructions on page 188

YAJILIN
EXTRA 2

	2↓	2↓	1↓			0↓	2↓	2↓
2→								
1→								
1→								
2→								
2→								
2→								

EXTRA INSTRUCTIONS

Some clue squares are empty. Treat them as if they were normal clue squares in terms of solving – i.e. do not count them as shaded squares.

WPC 2017 R3 Q20

YAJILIN
TRANSPARENT 1

2 →							← 2
	3 →				0↓	2↓	
	3 →						
				← 0			
			← 0				
						2↑	
	2↑	1↓				2↑	
1 →							← 1

EXTRA INSTRUCTIONS

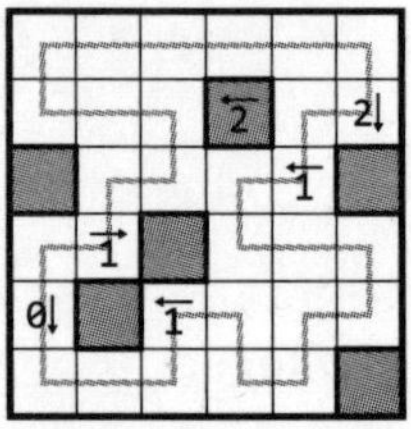

You can now shade clue squares too, and the loop must pass through <u>all</u> unshaded squares – even those containing clues. Shaded clues need no longer be fulfilled (although they might still be correct).

WPC 2017 R4 Q9

Instructions on page 188

YAJILIN
TRANSPARENT 2

EXTRA INSTRUCTIONS

You can now shade clue squares too, and the loop must pass through <u>all</u> unshaded squares – even those containing clues. Shaded clues need no longer be fulfilled (although they might still be correct).

WPC 2017 R4 Q9

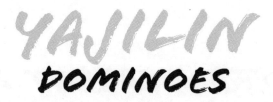

YAJILIN

DOMINOES

			1↓								1↓
							2→				
					3←					1↓	
					0↑						
	1↓					0↑		1↑			
								1↑	0→		
											1↑

EXTRA INSTRUCTIONS

Shade in dominoes (1×2 or 2×1 regions) instead of single squares. Clues now reveal the number of dominoes in the given direction, not the number of shaded squares. Dominoes cannot touch, except diagonally.

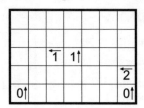

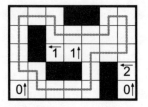

WPC 2013 R6 Q2

Instructions on page 188

17.
SPRINT ROUND

SPRINT
INSTRUCTIONS

World Puzzle Championships are divided into rounds, each typically lasting anywhere between 30 minutes and 2 hours.

At the 2014 World Puzzle Championship, the sixth round was a 'Sprint' round, consisting of 19 puzzles that the organisers thought that the best contestants would take around 30 minutes to solve.

In the event, the very best competitor managed to finish 18 of the 19 puzzles in the half hour of time. And now is *your* chance to see if you can do better, by playing the round exactly as it appeared in the competition.

To take part in the same way the competitors did, you first need to read the instruction booklet for the round, which starts on the following page. This sets out the instructions for each puzzle, and you can spend as long as you like reading this and practising the example puzzles.

Then, when you're ready, set aside 30 minutes when you won't be disturbed and sit down with a pencil, eraser, scrap paper (if you think you might need it) and any other pens you want – but no calculator, smart phone, smart watch, computer or any other assistance. Then, start a timer, and get solving!

Thirty minutes later, stop writing. Compare your solutions against the ones at the back of the book and see how many you got correct. If you have completed 15 or more, then congratulations! You're at the level of the top 50 solvers in the world. And if you solved them all, then you could be a world champion in waiting...

1. & 2. Number link

Draw a series of separate paths, each connecting a pair of identical numbers. No more than one line can enter any square, and lines can only travel horizontally or vertically between square centres.

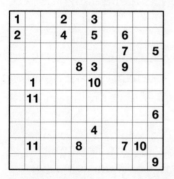 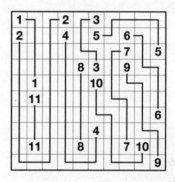

3. Fences

Draw a loop that visits every dot. The loop cannot cross or touch itself at any point. Only horizontal and vertical lines between dots are allowed. Some parts of the loop are already given.

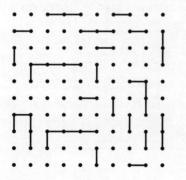 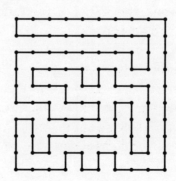

INSTRUCTION BOOKLET

4. Rectangles

Draw solid lines along some of the dashed lines in order to divide the grid up into a set of rectangles, such that every number is inside exactly one rectangle. The number inside each rectangle must be exactly equal to the number of grid squares that the rectangle contains. All grid squares are used.

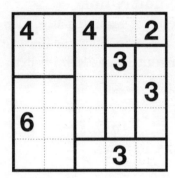

5. Yajilin

Draw a single loop using only horizontal and vertical lines such that the loop does not visit any square more than once. Any squares which the loop does not visit must be shaded. Shaded squares cannot touch orthogonally. Numbers with arrows indicate the exact number of shaded squares in a given direction in a specific row or column, but not all shaded squares are necessarily identified with arrows.

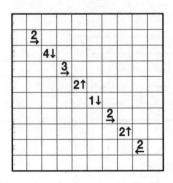
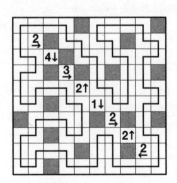

INSTRUCTION BOOKLET

6. Hashi

Join circled numbers with horizontal or vertical lines. Each number must have as many lines connected to it as specified by its value. No more than two lines may join any pair of numbers. No lines may cross. The finished layout must allow you to travel from any number to any other number just by following one or more lines.

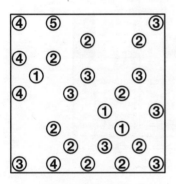 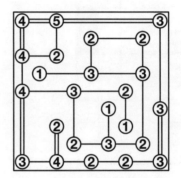

7. & 8. Slalom

Draw a diagonal line through each square. Diagonal lines never form a closed loop. Numbers in circles indicate the number of lines connected to that circle.

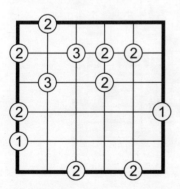 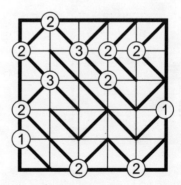

INSTRUCTION BOOKLET

9. & 10. Unequal Length Maze

Find a path from the bottom left to the top right passing through every empty square exactly once. The path must alternate horizontal and vertical segments, and no two consecutive segments can be the same length.

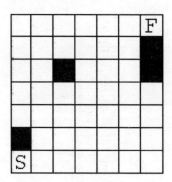 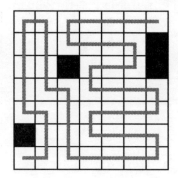

11. & 12. Walls

Draw a single horizontal or vertical line across the full width or height of the centre of every white square, such that the total length of all lines touching each black square is equal to the given number of squares.

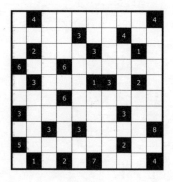 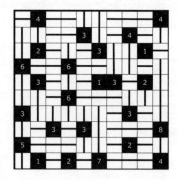

INSTRUCTION BOOKLET

13. & 14. Slitherlink

Draw a single loop by connecting together some dots so that each numbered square has the specified number of adjacent line segments. Dots can only be joined by straight horizontal or vertical lines. The loop cannot touch, cross or overlap itself in any way.

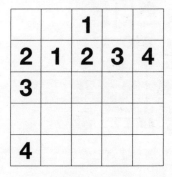 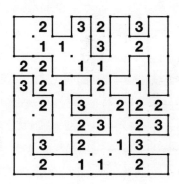

15 - 16. Toroidal Numberlink

Draw a series of separate paths, each connecting a pair of identical numbers. Paths are drawn by joining neighbouring square centres, not including diagonally neighbouring squares. No more than one path can enter any square. Paths can travel off one end of a row or column and re-enter at the opposite end of the same row or column, respectively.

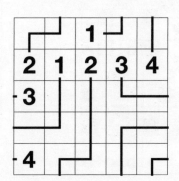

INSTRUCTION BOOKLET

17. Tapa

Shade some squares to create a continuous wall. Numbers in a square indicate the length of shaded square blocks in its neighbouring squares. If there is more than one number in a square there must be at least one unshaded square between the shaded square blocks. Shaded squares cannot form a 2×2 square or larger. There are no wall segments on squares containing numbers.

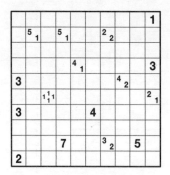 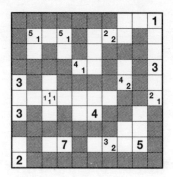

18 - 19. No Four in a Row

Place either an 'X' or an 'O' into each empty square such that four consecutive 'X's or 'O's do not appear horizontally, vertically or diagonally.

X	X	X			X	
				O		O
O						O
						O
O	X				O	
	X	X		O	O	
	X			O	O	O

X	X	X	O	X	X	X
X	O	X	X	O	O	O
O	X	O	O	O	X	O
O	O	X	X	O	X	O
O	X	X	O	X	O	X
X	X	X	O	O	O	X
O	X	O	X	O	O	O

Now stop reading. Do not start the following puzzles until you are ready to try your 30-minute competition round!

SPRINT
1. NUMBERLINK

1								2	3
							4		
	2		5		3				1
	6		4					6	
	7				7		5		
							8		
		8							

WPC 2014 R6 Q1

2. NUMBERLINK

1																	
			2													2	
		3					4	5									
									6								
			7										8			9	
		5					3										
			10					7									
	11				12						13	8					
													13				
		14		11										15	9		
16						10	12										15
			16						1		14			4			6

WPC 2014 R6 Q2

Instructions on page 201

SPRINT
3. FENCES

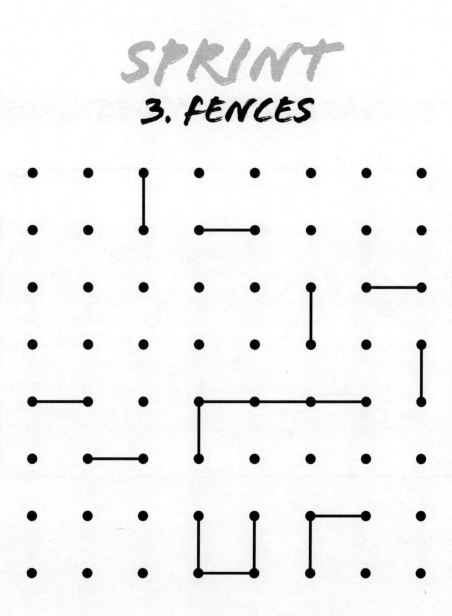

WPC 2014 R6 Q3

4. RECTANGLES

```
    7         10                              3
5           3                          12
        5   4              7
                    10         4              4
            4                      6
   15                  9          7
            3                      3
                5   8
       12                          5      10
  9        7
           5   2          8
10          7              7
```

5. YAJILIN

WPC 2014 R6 Q5

SPRINT
6. HASHI

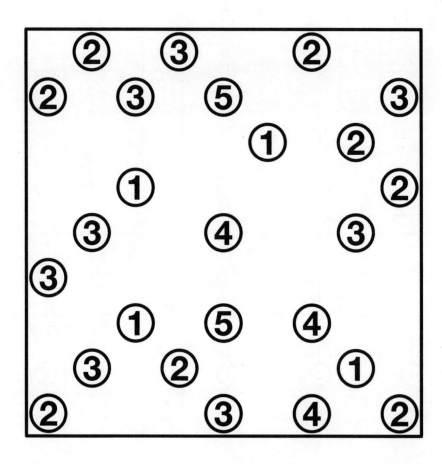

WPC 2014 R6 Q6

Instructions on page 203

7. SLALOM

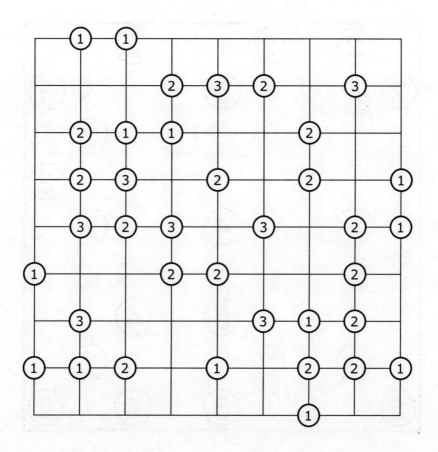

WPC 2014 R6 Q7

8. SLALOM

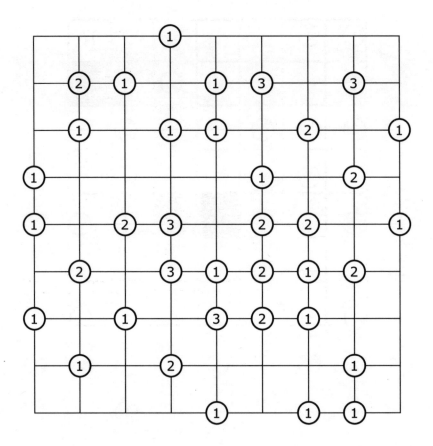

WPC 2014 R6 Q8

Instructions on page 203

9. UNEQUAL LENGTH MAZE

WPC 2014 R6 Q9

SPRINT
10. UNEQUAL LENGTH MAZE

WPC 2014 R6 Q10

Instructions on page 204

11. WALLS

	7		4			7			
									4
		4		4			3		
3			1						
					5		2		5
1		4							
					6			5	
	4			3					
			2			6			3
2		4			2		5		

WPC 2014 R6 Q11

12. WALLS

2		2		4				6	
			6						
7					1	1			
		1					6		6
					1				
	5			7			4		
		4							
6						5			4
		8							
2						4		7	

WPC 2014 R6 Q12

Instructions on page 204

13. SLITHERLINK

```
.   .   .   .   .   .   .   .   .   .
  3       3       3       2       3
.   .   .   .   .   .   .   .   .   .
      1   2       1       3
.   .   .   .   .   .   .   .   .   .
              3       1       1
.   .   .   .   .   .   .   .   .   .
      3       2       3
.   .   .   .   .   .   .   .   .   .
      1       2   0       3
.   .   .   .   .   .   .   .   .   .
      3       2   2       3
.   .   .   .   .   .   .   .   .   .
          1       2       3
.   .   .   .   .   .   .   .   .   .
  2       2       2
.   .   .   .   .   .   .   .   .   .
      1       3       2   1
.   .   .   .   .   .   .   .   .   .
  0   2       3       3       1
.   .   .   .   .   .   .   .   .   .
```

WPC 2014 R6 Q13

SPRINT
14. SLITHERLINK

```
.   .   .   .   .   .   .   .   .   .
    3   3           1   2       2
.   .   .   .   .   .   .   .   .   .
    1   1                   3
.   .   .   .   .   .   .   .   .   .
  3               1       1       1
.   .   .   .   .   .   .   .   .   .
    1   2           3
.   .   .   .   .   .   .   .   .   .
            3       2       3       2
.   .   .   .   .   .   .   .   .   .
  3       2       1       3
.   .   .   .   .   .   .   .   .   .
            2               2   0
.   .   .   .   .   .   .   .   .   .
  1       2       1               3
.   .   .   .   .   .   .   .   .   .
    3                       2   3
.   .   .   .   .   .   .   .   .   .
  3       3   3           1   2
.   .   .   .   .   .   .   .   .   .
```

WPC 2014 R6 Q14

Instructions on page 205

SPRINT
15. TOROIDAL NUMBERLINK

1	2	3	4	
		5	1	
2			3	
5		4		

WPC 2014 R6 Q15

SPRINT
16. TOROIDAL NUMBERLINK

1				
2	3		1	3
			4	
	4	2		

WPC 2014 R6 Q16

Instructions on page 205

17. TAPA

		2							
						²3		¹4	
		7							
¹₂²									
					8		¹5		
¹5		²3							
								7	
					7				
¹5		6							
					¹2				

WPC 2014 R6 Q17

SPRINT
18. NO FOUR IN A ROW

	O	X				O		O	X
	O						O		O
X			X	X					
		X		X					O
O					X	X		X	
		X	X						
O				X					X
		X			X		X		
X	X			O					X
	X	X	O	O					O

WPC 2014 R6 Q18

Instructions on page 206

SPRINT
19. NO FOUR IN A ROW

		X					O	O	O
	O		O	X		O	X	O	
O			O					X	O
	O		O						
							O		X
O	O				O			X	
O						O			X
	X			X					
O			X						
O	O		O	X	X		X	O	X

WPC 2014 R6 Q19

18.
THE GREAT OUTDOORS

OUTDOORS
INSTRUCTIONS

At the 2014 World Puzzle Championship, held in London for the first time since the championships began in New York back in 1992, the third round was full of novel loop puzzles, all linked via the theme 'The Great Outdoors' (or 'Outdoors' as these pages are headed, for reasons of space).

In all of the puzzles in this round, the aim is to draw a loop ('trail') that travels all around 'the great outdoors', visiting every square except for those with trees in (and occasionally other obstacles too).

Contestants were given 30 minutes to complete the puzzles in this round, and just under 40 competitors succeeded in doing just that. The fastest time went to Japanese A-team player Ken Endo, who finished after just 13 minutes – an incredibly quick time! The fastest UK competitor was Neil Zussman, who successfully completed the round in just under 23 minutes.

To try the round under competition conditions, start by reading the instruction booklet that begins on the following page. You can spend as long as you like reading this and practising the example puzzles. Then, when you're ready, time yourself solving for 30 minutes – without the help of a phone, computer or any other aid.

When thirty minutes is up, stop writing. Compare your solutions against the ones at the back of the book and see how you did. Did you get near the performance of the world's best solvers?

OUTDOORS
INSTRUCTION BOOKLET

1. Woodland Trail

Draw a trail which starts and ends at the flag in the top left corner of the grid and visits every square except for those occupied by a tree. The trail moves left/right/up/down between the centres of squares and does not touch or cross itself.

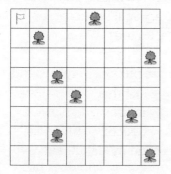 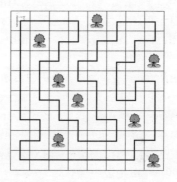

Continued overleaf

INSTRUCTION BOOKLET

2. Numbered Trail

Draw a trail which starts at the flag in the top left corner of the grid, visits every numbered viewpoint in numerical order, then returns to the flag. Every square must be visited except for those occupied by a tree. The trail moves left/right/up/down between the centres of squares and does not touch or cross itself.

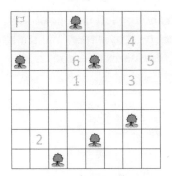

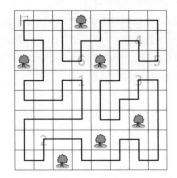

3. Riverside Trail

Draw a trail which starts and ends at the flag in the top left corner of the grid and visits every square except for those occupied by a tree. The trail moves left/right/up/down between the centres of squares and does not touch or cross itself. The river, shown by a bold line, can only be crossed at the given bridges. There is no requirement to cross every bridge.

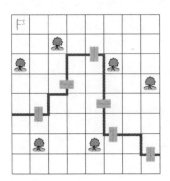

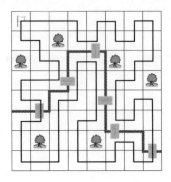

INSTRUCTION BOOKLET

4. Campsite Trail

Place a tent in one of the squares sharing a side with each tree. Squares occupied by tents cannot touch each other even at a corner. Then draw a trail which starts and ends at the flag in the top left corner of the grid and visits every square except for those occupied by trees or tents. The trail moves left/right/up/down between the centres of squares and does not touch or cross itself.

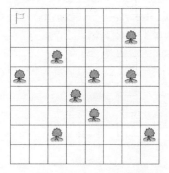
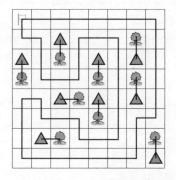

Continued overleaf

INSTRUCTION BOOKLET

5. Mountain Trail

Draw a trail which starts and ends at the flag in the top left corner of the grid and visits every square except for those occupied by a tree. The trail moves left/right/up/down between the centres of squares and does not touch or cross itself. The grid is divided into 3 regions by shading. Lighter shading represents the lower slopes of a mountain and darker shading represents the summit region of the mountain. The trail starts and finishes in the unshaded lowland region and makes a single ascent of the mountain and a single descent i.e. the trail has only 5 sections: lowland, lower slopes, summit region, lower slopes, lowland.

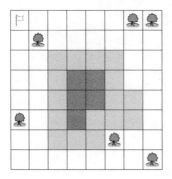
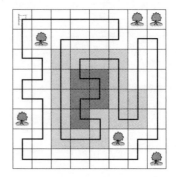

INSTRUCTION BOOKLET

6. Running Trail

Draw a trail which starts and ends at the flag in the top left corner of the grid and visits every square except for those occupied by a tree. The trail moves left/right/up/down between the centres of squares and does not touch or cross itself. The trail is divided into sections of equal length. Each intermediate checkpoint is marked by a flag.

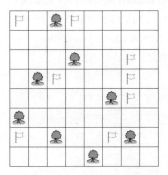 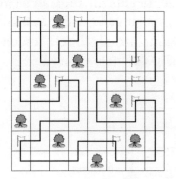

Continued overleaf

INSTRUCTION BOOKLET

7. Farm Trail

The grid represents a farm that is divided into fields. Certain squares are occupied by an animal and these squares cannot touch by a side. The number of animals in each field is given. Work out the positions of the animals and draw a trail which starts and ends at the flag in the top left corner of the grid and visits every square except for those occupied by a tree or an animal. The trail moves left/right/up/down between the centres of squares and does not touch or cross itself. Once the trail leaves the first field, it enters the remaining fields exactly once each before returning to the first field again.

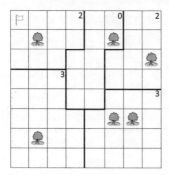 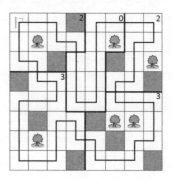

Now stop reading. Do not start the following puzzles until you are ready to try your 30-minute competition round!

OUTDOORS
1. WOODLAND TRAIL

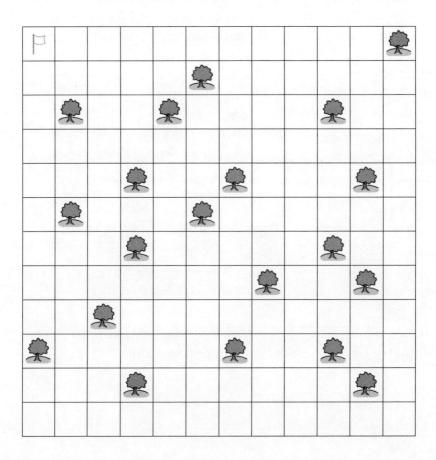

WPC 2014 R2 Q1

OUTDOORS
2. NUMBERED TRAIL

WPC 2014 R2 Q2

Instructions on page 230

OUTDOORS
3. RIVERSIDE TRAIL

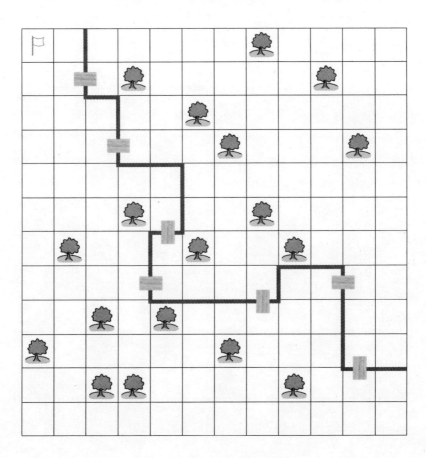

WPC 2014 R2 Q3

OUTDOORS
4. CAMPSITE TRAIL

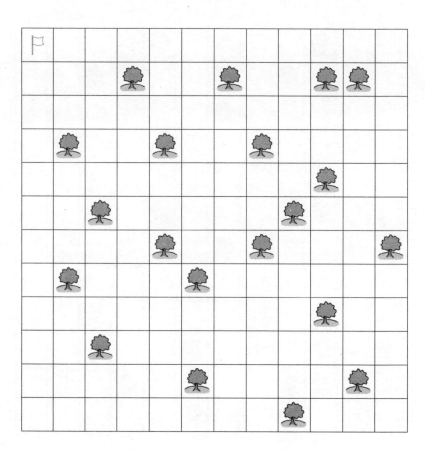

WPC 2014 R2 Q4

Instructions on page 231

OUTDOORS
5. MOUNTAIN TRAIL

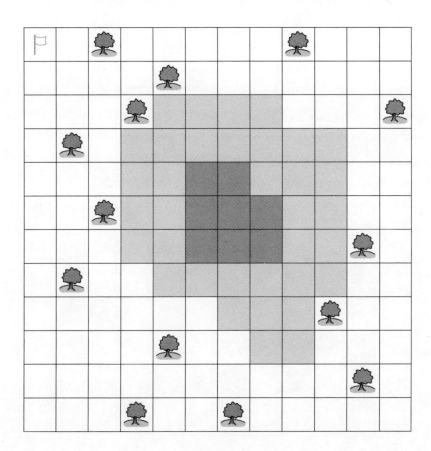

WPC 2014 R2 Q5

OUTDOORS
6. RUNNING TRAIL

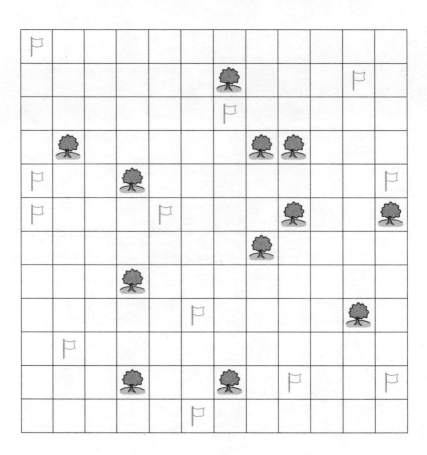

WPC 2014 R2 Q6

Instructions on page 233

OUTDOORS
7. FARM TRAIL

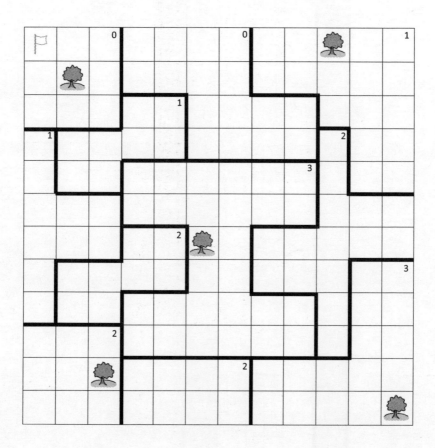

WPC 2014 R2 Q7

19.
WELCOME

WELCOME
INSTRUCTIONS

Now, after 18 chapters of practice and preparation, you're ready to compete for real. This is your final chance to see how you compare with the best in the world.

Welcome to the first round of the 2014 World Puzzle Championship, appropriately entitled 'Welcome'.

This round consists of a mix of 15 puzzles, with only 3 types which you will have previously encountered in this book – and so it will provide a real test of your puzzling skills.

The competitors in the actual competition were given 50 minutes to complete the round under examination conditions, but you can take as long as you like. If you really want to simulate the exam conditions, then you should sit at a one-person desk in a large hall, and start solving at exactly 9:10am, just as the competitors did.

Once you are done, you can compare your time with the fastest solver of this round, and arguably the greatest puzzle solver ever, Ulrich Voigt. He is a regular member of the elite German A-team, and has been crowned World Puzzle Champion a staggering eleven times (as of 2017).

Ulrich completed this round in just under 44 minutes. How quickly can you solve it?

WELCOME

INSTRUCTION BOOKLET

1. Suraromu

Draw a single loop that passes through every gate in numerical order. The puzzle contains 'x' dashed-line gates, each of which can be travelled through only once. Some gates are numbered, 'n', and must be passed through as the 'n'th gate in the loop. The loop cannot enter any square more than once, and can only travel horizontally or vertically. Between the 'x'th and 1st gates the loop must travel through the square containing the circled number, which is equal to the number of gates, 'x'. Numbered gates have numbers on both sides of the gate, except if the gate touches the edge of the puzzle in which case it has a single number. The line must pass straight through a gate, so cannot turn on a gate square.

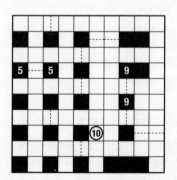 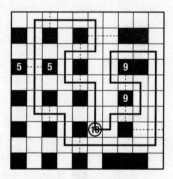

INSTRUCTION BOOKLET

2. Fillomino

Fill each empty square with a number such that every number in the grid is part of a continuous region of that many squares. A region is continuous whenever two squares touch by a side. Two different regions made up of the same number of squares cannot touch by a side.

	4	1	5
3	2	1	

4	4	1	5
3	4	4	5
3	2	5	5
3	2	1	5

3. & 4. Akari

Place light bulbs in some white squares so that every white square is illuminated. Light bulbs illuminate every white square in their row and column directions until blocked by a black square. No light bulb can be illuminated by another light bulb. Clue numbers correspond to the number of light bulbs in the four squares that share a side.

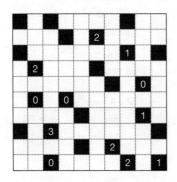

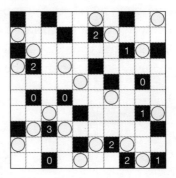

INSTRUCTION BOOKLET

5. Striped Snake

Shade squares to form a snake which cannot touch itself, not even diagonally. (A snake is a one-square wide path through a grid – see the example solution to clarify this). All odd squares of the snake are black and all even squares are grey. Clues at the left show the number of black squares in the corresponding row. Clues on the top show the number of grey squares in the corresponding column. The head and tail of the snake are shown as black squares.

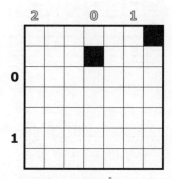 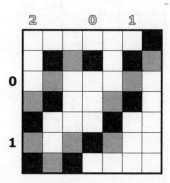

6. Pentominos

Place the complete set of pentominos (a smaller set in the example) into the grid. Pentominos can be rotated and reflected. Pentominos cannot touch each other, not even at a corner. Clues outside the grid show the number of empty squares before the first pentomino is reached.

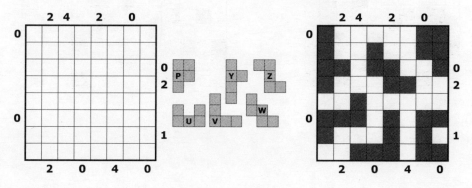

INSTRUCTION BOOKLET

7. Dominoes

A standard set of 28 dominoes has been placed in the grid. Mark the position of each domino.

4	6	2	5	5	2	0	1
0	4	4	0	0	1	6	3
2	4	4	1	1	3	1	5
2	5	0	2	2	2	0	0
5	3	3	6	4	1	3	5
1	4	1	4	5	6	6	5
6	6	3	0	3	3	6	2

0 0	0 1	0 2	0 3	0 4	0 5	0 6
	1 1	1 2	1 3	1 4	1 5	1 6
		2 2	2 3	2 4	2 5	2 6
			3 3	3 4	3 5	3 6
				4 4	4 5	4 6
					5 5	5 6
						6 6

4	6	2	5	5	2	0	1
0	4	4	0	0	1	6	3
2	4	4	1	1	3	1	5
2	5	0	2	2	2	0	0
5	3	3	6	4	1	3	5
1	4	1	4	5	6	6	5
6	6	3	0	3	3	6	2

8. Tents

Attach a tent to each tree, in a horizontally or vertically touching square. Squares with tents do not touch each other, not even diagonally. Numbers outside the grid indicate the number of tents in that row or column.

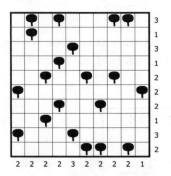

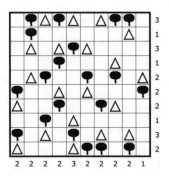

INSTRUCTION BOOKLET

9. & 10. Tri-minesweeper

Place 14 right-angled triangles (7 in the example) into some empty squares in the grid. Each triangle occupies exactly half a square. Triangles cannot touch each other, not even at a point. Clues in squares show the number of triangles touching that square, including only at a point.

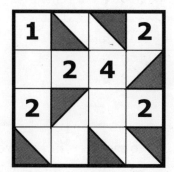

11. & 12. Magic Summer

Place the digits 2, 0, 1 and 4 once each into every row and column. Each continuous block of two or more digits in a row or column is considered a multiple-digit number. Multiple-digit numbers cannot start with '0'. Clues outside the grid give the total of all numbers in that row or column.

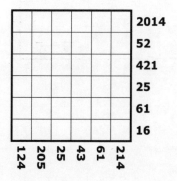

INSTRUCTION BOOKLET

13. & 14. Digitile

Place the digits 2, 0, 1 and 4 into the grid by drawing along some grid lines. You can use each digit any number of times. Digits cannot touch each other, even at a point. Clues to the left/top of the grid show the number of digits in the corresponding row or column. Clues to the right/bottom show the sum of the digits in the corresponding row or column. Digits can be rotated but otherwise must be drawn exactly as shown, and not resized in any way. A digit is counted as being 'in' a row or column if one or more of the lines making up that digit crosses that row or column.

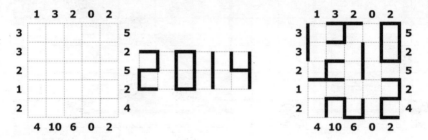

15. Scramble UK

Place all the given words in the grid so that they form a single interlocking crossword. All words must read either from left to right or from top to bottom and no words can appear which are not in the list. Every shaded square must contain either a U or a K and neither of these letters can appear in any unshaded square.

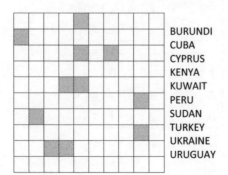

BURUNDI
CUBA
CYPRUS
KENYA
KUWAIT
PERU
SUDAN
TURKEY
UKRAINE
URUGUAY

Do not proceed to the next page until you are ready to start the timer.

WELCOME
1. SURAKOMU

WPC 2014 R1 Q1

WELCOME
2. FILLOMINO

3			3		4			4	
3			5		5		2		
2			1		**20**	5			
3			5		**14**	3			
5			4		2		4		
1	**20**	**14**	1			3		5	

WPC 2014 R1 Q2

Instructions on page 246

WELCOME

3. AKARI

WPC 2014 R1 Q3

WELCOME

4. AKARI

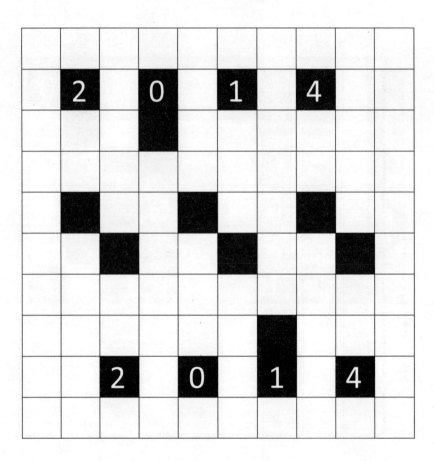

WPC 2014 R1 Q4

Instructions on page 246

WELCOME
5. STRIPED SNAKE

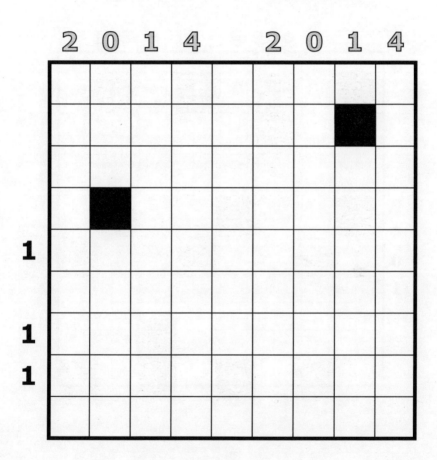

WPC 2014 R1 Q5

WELCOME
6. PENTOMINOS

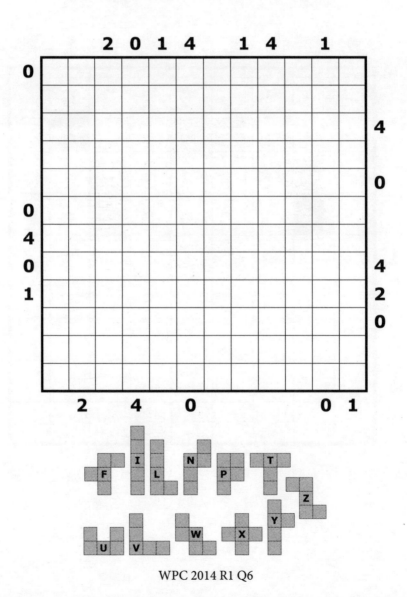

WPC 2014 R1 Q6

Instructions on page 247

WELCOME
7. DOMINOES

	2	0	1	4			
5	5	5	5	3	2	2	6
2	5	6	6	■	■	2	2	4	2
0	1	■	6	6	3	3	■	6	0
1	1	■	4	0	0	0	■	3	1
4	4	3	1	■	■	6	5	3	4
	4	0	1	3	6	5	5	3
	2	0	1	4	

0 0	0 1	0 2	0 3	0 4	0 5	0 6
	1 1	1 2	1 3	1 4	1 5	1 6
		2 2	2 3	2 4	2 5	2 6
			3 3	3 4	3 5	3 6
				4 4	4 5	4 6
					5 5	5 6
						6 6

WPC 2014 R1 Q7

WELCOME

8. TENTS

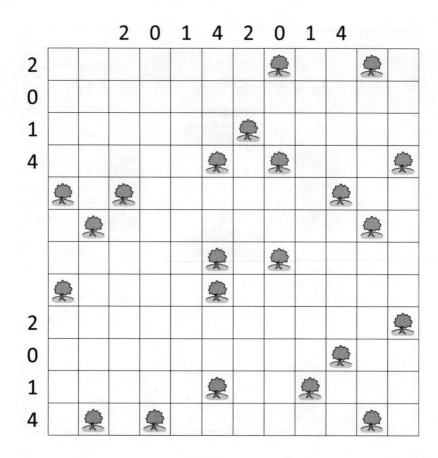

WPC 2014 R1 Q8

Instructions on page 248

WELCOME
9. TRI-MINESWEEPER

						2
	2		0			
		0			0	
1			1			
				4		
	4					
					2	

WPC 2014 R1 Q9

WELCOME
10. TRI-MINESWEEPER

					1
	2				2
		0			
			1		
		2		4	
				2	

WPC 2014 R1 Q10

Instructions on page 249

WELCOME
11. MAGIC SUMMER

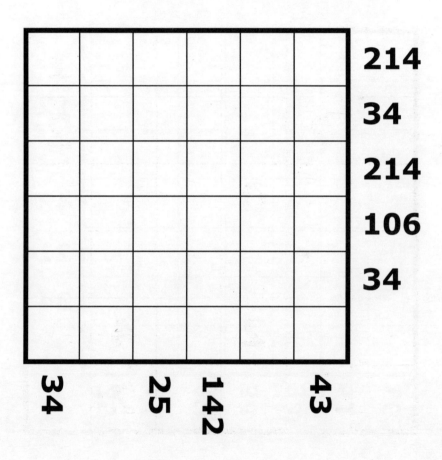

214

34

214

106

34

34 25 142 43

WPC 2014 R1 Q11

WELCOME
12. MAGIC SUMMER

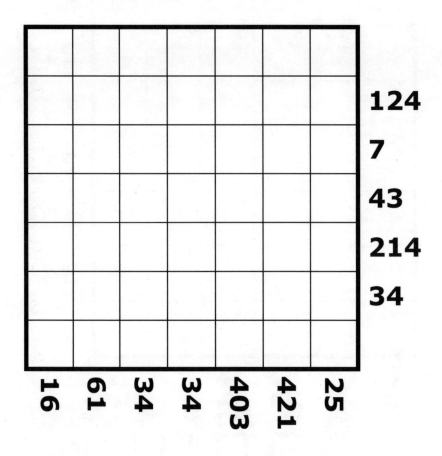

WPC 2014 R1 Q12

Instructions on page 249

13. DIGITILE

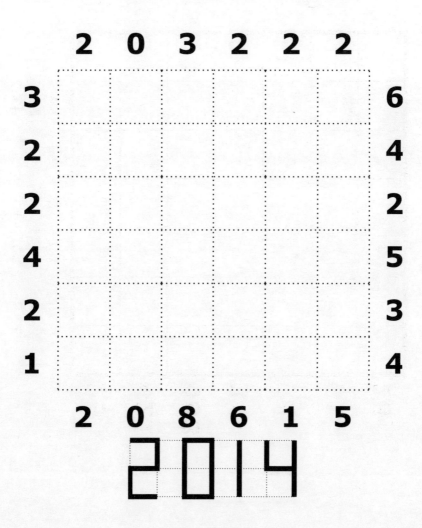

WPC 2014 R1 Q13

WELCOME

14. DIGITILE

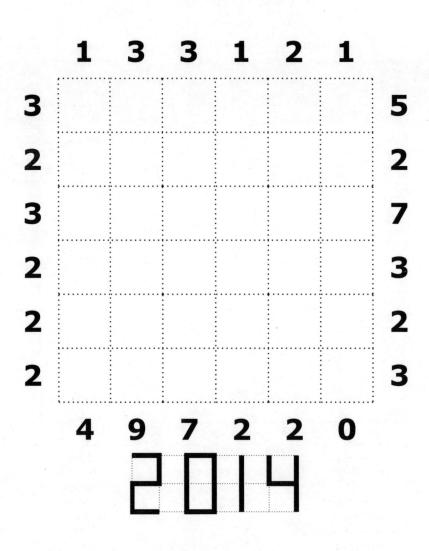

WPC 2014 R1 Q14

Instructions on page 250

WELCOME
15. SCRAMBLE UK

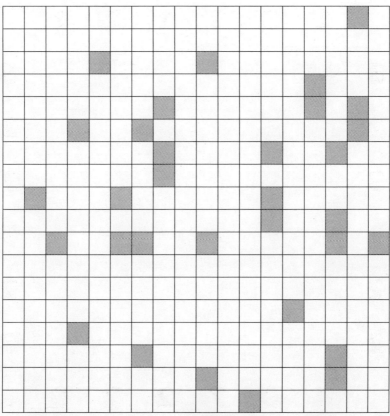

AKARI	KAKURO	PUZZLE
ARUKONE	KEISUKE	SHAKASHAKA
CLOUDS	KENKEN	SHIKAKU
FOURWINDS	KROPKI	SKYSCRAPERS
FUTOSHIKI	KURODOKU	SLITHERLINK
HASHIWOKAKERO	MASYU	SUDOKU
HEYAWAKE	NURIKABE	SURAROMU

WPC 2014 R1 Q15

20.
SOLUTIONS

SOLUTIONS

Page 17

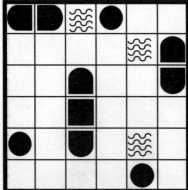

Page 18

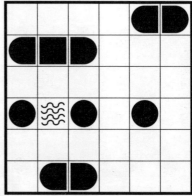

Page 19

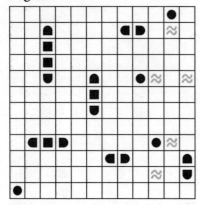

Page 20

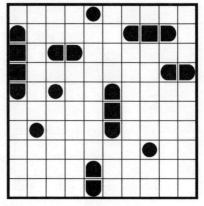

Page 21

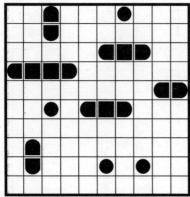

Page 22

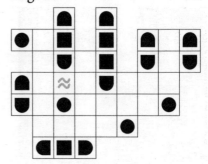

SOLUTIONS

Page 23

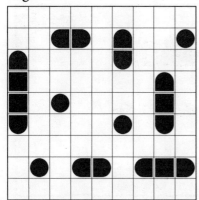

Page 24

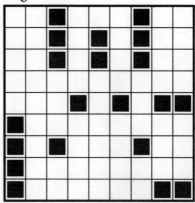

Page 25

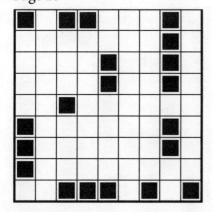

Page 26

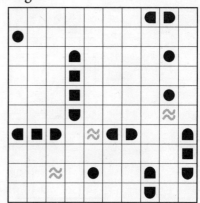

Page 29

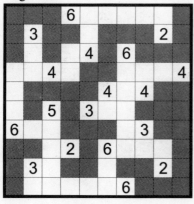

Page 30

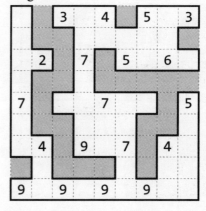

SOLUTIONS

Page 31

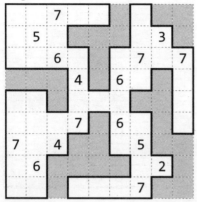

Page 32

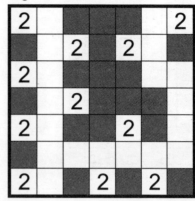

Page 33

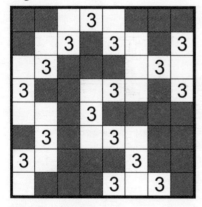

Page 34

Page 35

Page 36

2	4	6	2	4	3	6	4
7	5	3	4	7	5	5	2
5	4	8	6	3	2	5	8
4	6	5	2	5	6	4	2
7	4	4	7	8	6	5	4
4	4	2	5	3	6	3	3
3	5	5	8	6	5	6	7
5	3	2	5	3	4	2	9

SOLUTIONS

Page 39

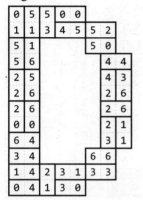

Page 40

4	5	5	6	6	3	1	4	7
6	1	2	3	2	2	2	1	1
1	0	0	0	3	3	1	1	6
6	0	4	3	7	6	7	3	2
6	0	2	4	7	7	7	2	1
1	0	0	0	7	5	7	2	3
3	4	5	4	5	5	4	2	6
0	3	5	6	5	4	4	5	7

Page 41

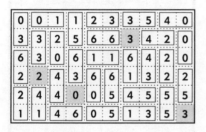

Page 42

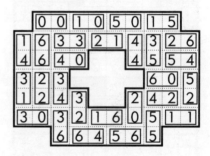

Page 43

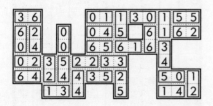

Page 44

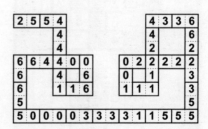

SOLUTIONS

Page 45

Page 46

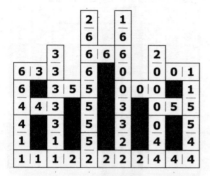

Page 49

Page 50

Page 51

Page 52

SOLUTIONS

Page 53

5	5	5	1	4	4	20	20	1	21	21
5	1	20	4	4	20	20	1	21	21	1
5	20	20	20	20	20	1	21	21	1	22
1	4	20	20	20	1	21	21	1	22	22
4	4	20	20	1	21	21	1	22	22	7
4	20	20	1	21	21	1	22	22	3	7
20	20	1	21	21	1	22	22	22	3	7
20	1	21	21	1	22	22	22	22	3	7
1	21	21	1	22	22	22	22	5	5	7
21	21	1	22	22	6	6	6	1	5	7
21	1	22	22	6	6	6	1	5	5	7

Page 54

19	19	19	19	19	19	19	19	19	19	19
19	2	1	3	1	19	6	6	6	5	19
1	2	5	3	3	2	2	6	5	5	19
5	5	5	2	2	11	11	6	5	5	19
5	4	3	3	3	11	14	6	14	19	19
1	4	11	11	11	11	14	14	14	14	19
3	4	11	11	11	11	1	14	4	4	4
3	4	5	5	5	2	2	14	14	3	4
3	5	5	1	14	14	14	14	14	3	3

Page 55

2	2	6	13	13	2	2	13	2	2	1
6	6	6	13	13	13	13	13	3	3	2
6	6	8	13	13	13	2	5	5	3	2
8	8	8	1	13	13	2	5	5	5	4
8	6	8	3	3	2	4	2	2	4	4
2	6	8	8	3	2	4	4	4	1	4
2	6	2	3	4	4	3	3	3	4	2
6	6	2	3	3	4	1	4	4	4	2
6	4	4	2	2	4	2	7	3	3	3
3	4	4	5	5	5	2	7	7	7	2
3	3	5	5	2	2	7	7	1	7	2

Page 56

44	44	44	44	17	17	17	17	17
44	44	44	44	44	44	44	44	17
44	4	4	4	4	44	44	44	17
44	44	44	44	8	8	44	44	17
44	4	4	4	4	8	44	44	17
44	44	44	44	8	8	44	44	17
44	4	4	4	4	8	8	8	17
44	44	44	44	44	44	44	44	17
44	44	44	44	17	17	17	17	17

Page 59

Page 60

SOLUTIONS

Page 61

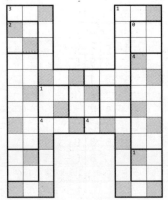

Page 62

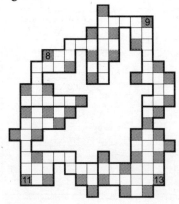

Page 63

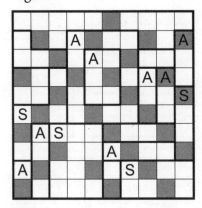

Page 64

4		3		3	3
					4
			1		
3		4			
		2		4
3		3		

Page 67

5	7	2	1	8	5	3	10	5	9
9	3	7	6	10	8	5	4	2	6
7	1	10	4	8	6	7	7	5	10
1	3	4	9	7	8	3	5	8	10
7	2	6	8	6	3	10	1	4	5
8	3	3	5	9	5	6	5	7	5
1	8	1	10	6	9	4	6	1	7
3	10	1	5	6	4	1	9	6	2
4	5	10	7	3	8	1	8	9	4
10	10	8	7	1	2	1	3	6	4

Page 68

6	6	9	7	3	1	8	1	3	6
2	3	7	6	9	7	1	8	4	1
5	4	2	3	4	6	9	5	8	5
7	8	4	4	2	10	10	9	10	6
6	10	7	8	9	4	7	10	9	3
8	9	8	5	7	8	1	5	10	4
4	10	3	9	4	5	7	1	9	8
8	2	4	8	3	6	6	4	1	5
5	9	8	2	4	10	3	6	10	9
4	7	5	6	8	7	4	3	6	3

SOLUTIONS

Page 69

6	2	8	9	4	6	8	6	4	10
1	5	6	10	3	4	2	9	2	8
3	4	1	8	1	3	1	10	5	7
5	9	10	4	9	6	2	5	4	10
4	6	8	1	10	9	1	7	3	2
3	9	6	2	8	4	4	1	6	3
6	5	1	5	4	8	1	2	5	4
3	8	2	10	1	7	6	5	10	3
10	7	10	3	8	1	9	7	8	10
8	6	4	6	5	2	4	3	7	9

Page 70

6	10	5	5	11	3	10	4	10	1	2	8
8	6	1	9	10	5	7	2	11	4	8	3
4	9	7	12	6	2	9	3	8	12	7	4
11	5	12	1	4	9	5	11	6	7	3	2
3	11	6	2	5	1	3	5	10	8	12	4
7	1	10	11	2	7	3	6	9	2	5	11
12	7	11	4	9	10	1	9	12	6	5	11
5	4	6	1	3	12	2	12	7	7	11	10
4	5	12	10	6	8	9	8	2	11	6	1
2	3	9	7	12	5	6	1	3	3	4	7
4	8	3	5	5	11	6	2	1	10	8	6
10	1	2	3	7	6	11	10	4	1	9	5

Page 71

1	1	4	3	4	1	3	2	2
1	1	2	3	2	1	3	2	2
3	2	1	4	3	3	2	1	3
4	3	4	2	3	1	1	2	4
4	2	1	1	2	3	3	4	1
2	2	3	3	4	4	4	1	2
2	3	3	1	3	2	2	4	1
4	4	2	1	3	1	2	3	3
4	4	2	1	1	1	2	3	3

Page 72

	1	2	3	5	4	7
1		3	9	7	2	4
2	4		1	3	9	5
3	8	4		6	1	2
4	5	8	2		7	1
7	6	5	4	2		3
6	2	9	5	1	3	

Page 73

3	9	6	2	5	1	6	8	7
6	1	2	7	3	3	4	9	5
7	3	9	8	6	9	7	2	5
3	7	5	1	8	4	2	7	8
9	8	8	6	7	4	5	1	4
1	5	9	3	5	8	1	6	4
5	4	1	2	2	6	8	7	9
2	2	3	5	4	3	6	5	1
4	6	8	7	1	9	7	3	2

Page 74

K	O	P	R	I	V	N	I	C	A
R	L	O	D	S	M	P	T	M	I
Y	P	J	U	L	V	P	E	K	W
D	M	I	A	B	B	J	Z	D	M
G	O	D	R	X	G	L	M	B	S
K	S	E	U	F	I	B	S	W	F
M	Q	A	V	R	B	T	Z	Q	S
N	I	V	H	B	A	I	K	N	H
V	L	D	S	M	J	K	F	B	J
W	P	C	C	R	O	A	T	I	A

SOLUTIONS

Page 77

Page 78

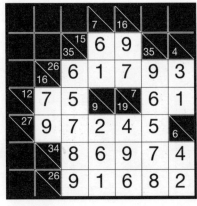

Page 79

Page 80

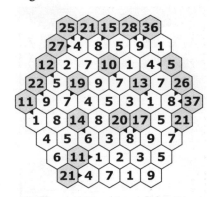

Page 81

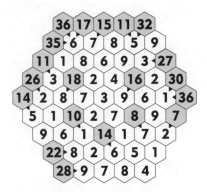

Page 82

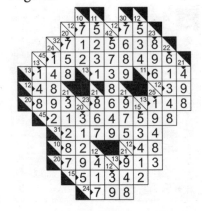

SOLUTIONS

Page 83

5	9	8	7	³⁄₆	2	0	4	1
7	1	³⁄₂	0	4	9	6	5	8
6	4	0	5	1	8	9	3	²⁄₇
3	0	6	8	7	¹⁄₅	4	2	9
²⁄₁	5	9	6	0	4	7	8	3
4	8	7	9	2	3	5	¹⁄₆	0
9	7	1	²⁄₃	5	6	8	0	4
8	2	5	4	9	0	¹⁄₃	7	6
0	³⁄₆	4	1	8	7	2	9	5

Page 84

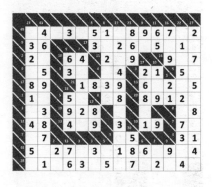

Page 87

3 2	8 7 6	4 5	1
4 1	5 3 2	6	8 7
7 5	3 4 1	8	6 2
8 3 2	5 4	7	1 6
2 8 1	6 7	5	3 4
1 7 6	2 8	3 4 5
5 6 4	1 3 2	7 8
6 4	7 8 5	1 2 3

Page 88

5	1	4	7	3	8	6	2
2	8	5	1	7	3 4	6
6 3	8 4 2 1	7	5
4	7	1	6	8	5	2 3
7 6 3	8	5	2 1	4
8	5	7	2	6	4 3	1
3 4 2	5	1	6	8 7
1 2	6 3 4	7	5	8

Page 89

5	4 3	8 7 6	1 2
8	3	7	1	6	2	5 4
6 5	1	7 8	4	2 3
7	2 4 3	5	8	6	1
1	6	2 4	3	7 8	5
2	1	8	5 4 3	7 6
3	7	5 6	2 1	4	8
4 8	6	2	1	5	3	7

Page 90

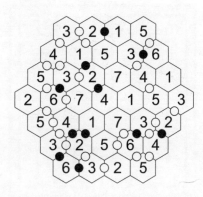

SOLUTIONS

Page 91

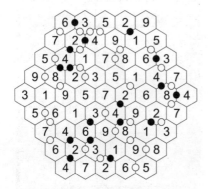

Page 92

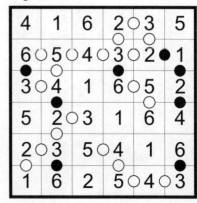

Page 93

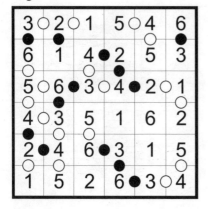

Page 94

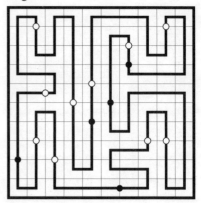

Page 95

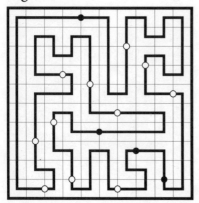

Page 96

SOLUTIONS

Page 99

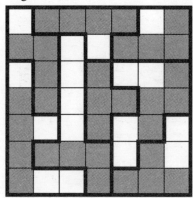

Page 100

Page 101

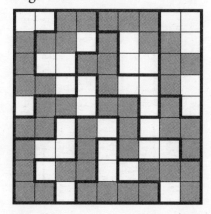

Page 102

Page 103

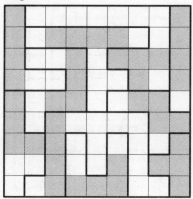

Page 104

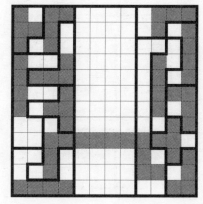

SOLUTIONS

Page 105

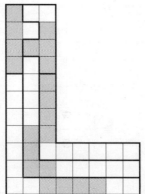

Page 106

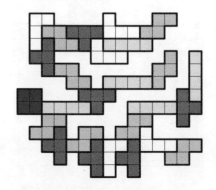

Page 107

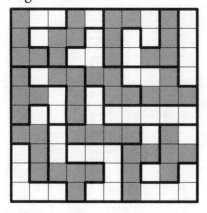

Page 108

Page 111

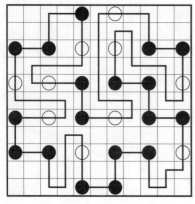

Page 112

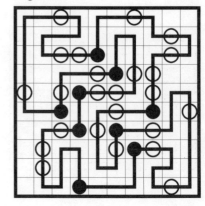

SOLUTIONS

Page 113

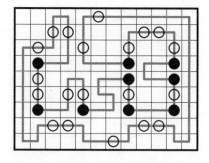

Page 114

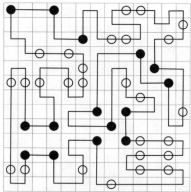

Page 115

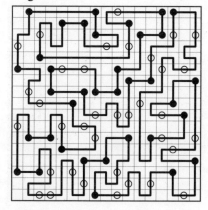

Page 116

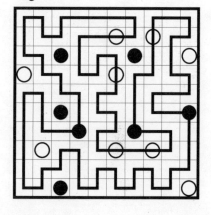

Page 117

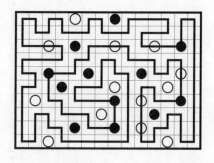

Page 118

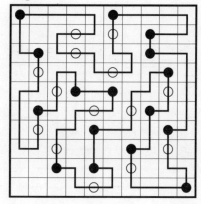

SOLUTIONS

Page 119

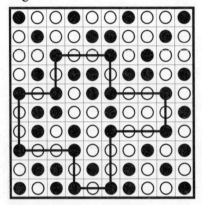

Page 120

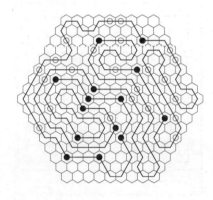

Page 123

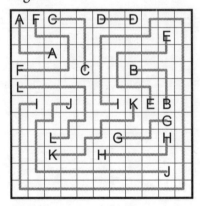

Page 124

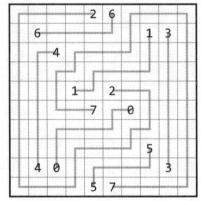

Page 125

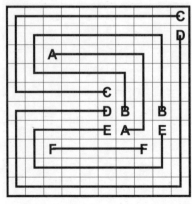

Page 126

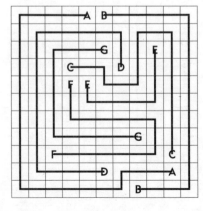

SOLUTIONS

Page 127

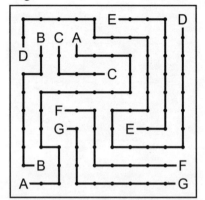

Page 128

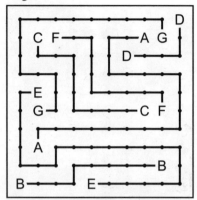

Page 129

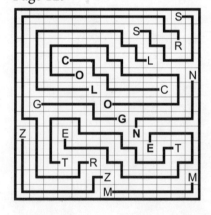

Page 130

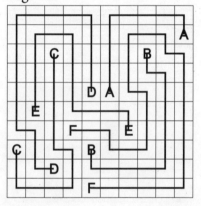

Page 131

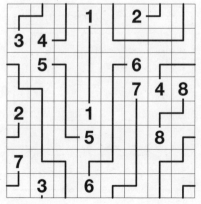

Page 132

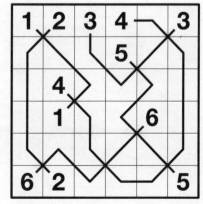

SOLUTIONS

Page 135

Page 136

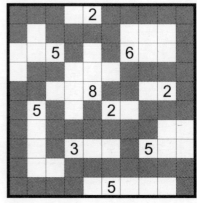

Page 137

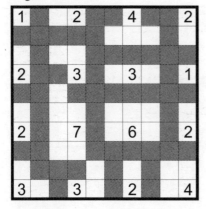

Page 138

Page 139

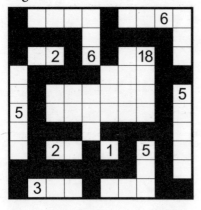

Page 140

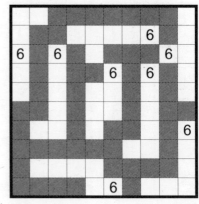

SOLUTIONS

Page 141

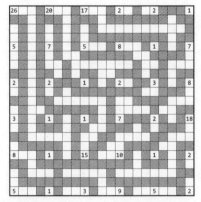

Page 142

Page 143

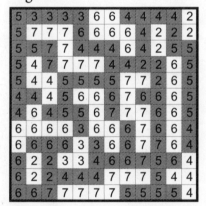

Page 144

Page 147

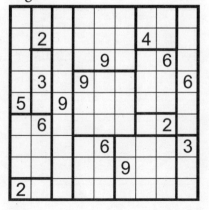

Page 148

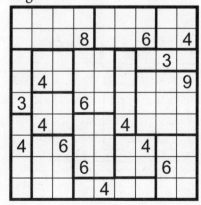

SOLUTIONS

Page 149

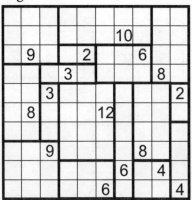

Page 150

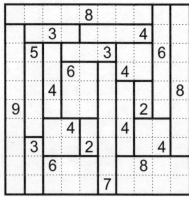

Page 151

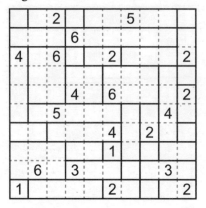

Page 152

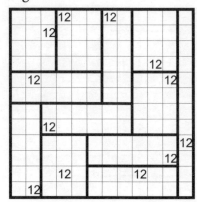

Page 153

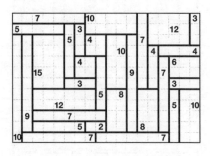

Page 154

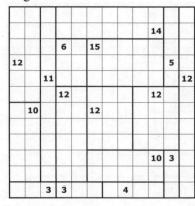

SOLUTIONS

Page 155

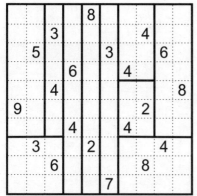

Page 156

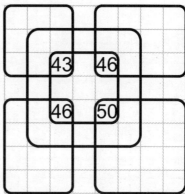

Page 157

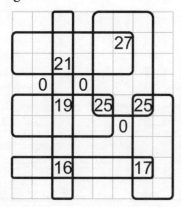

Page 158

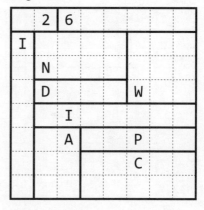

Page 161

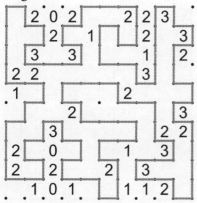

Page 162

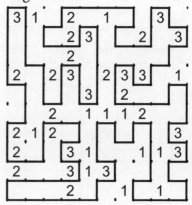

SOLUTIONS

Page 163

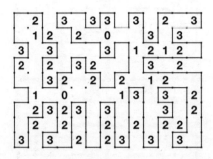

Page 164

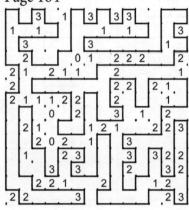

Page 165

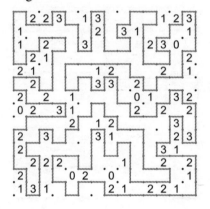

Page 166

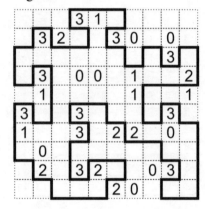

Page 167

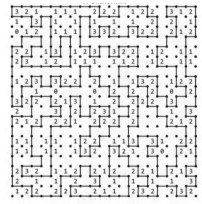

Page 168

SOLUTIONS

Page 169

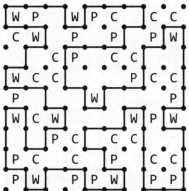

Page 170

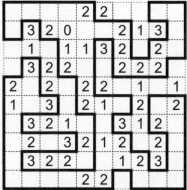

Page 171

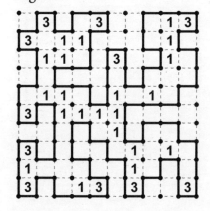

Page 172

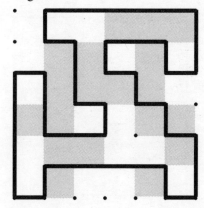

Page 173

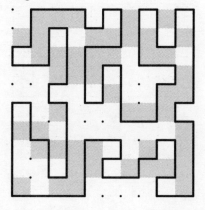

Page 174

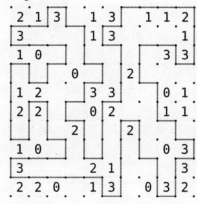

SOLUTIONS

Page 177

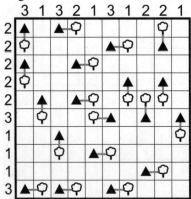

Page 178

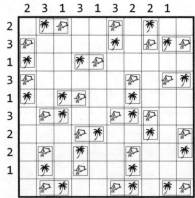

Page 179

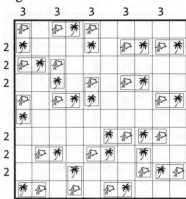

Page 180

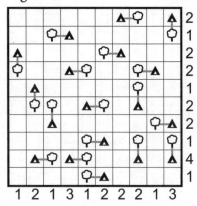

Page 181

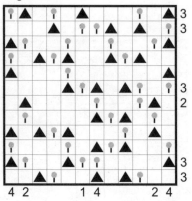

Page 182

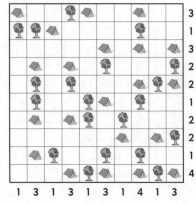

SOLUTIONS

Page 183

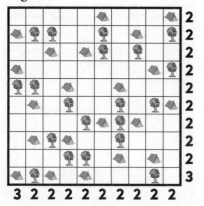

Page 184

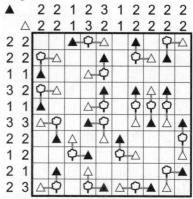

Page 185

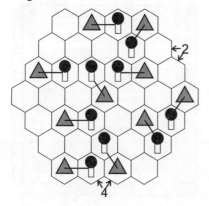

Page 186

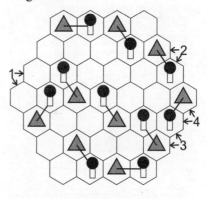

Page 189

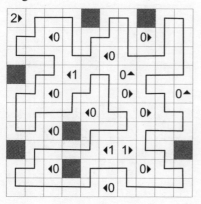

Page 190

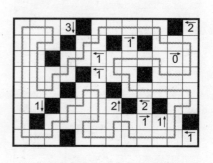

SOLUTIONS

Page 191

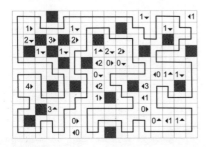

Page 192

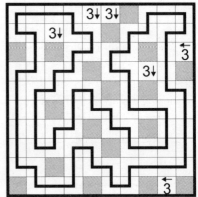

Page 193

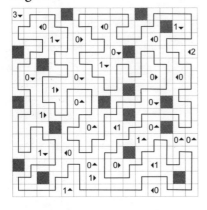

Page 194

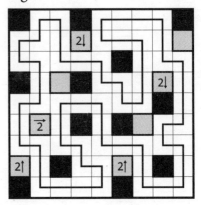

Page 195

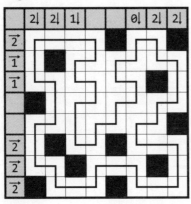

Page 196

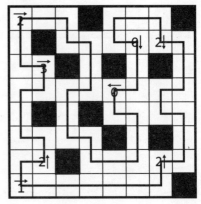

SOLUTIONS

Page 197

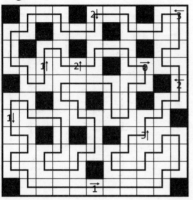

Page 198

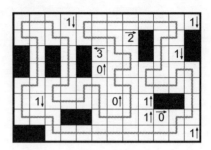

Page 207

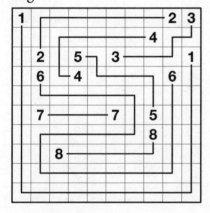

Page 208

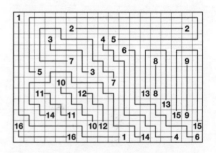

Page 209

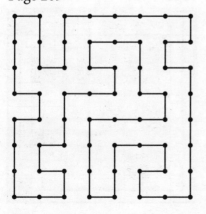

Page 210

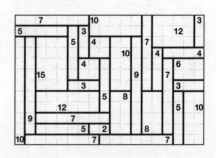

SOLUTIONS

Page 211

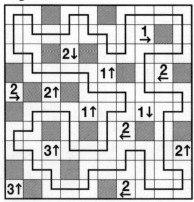

Page 212

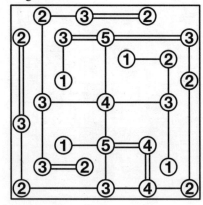

Page 213

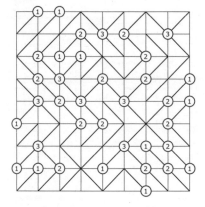

Page 214

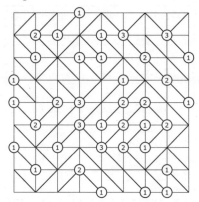

Page 215

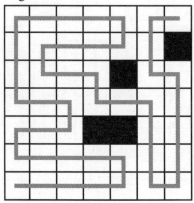

Page 216

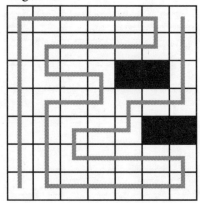

SOLUTIONS

Page 217

Page 218

Page 219

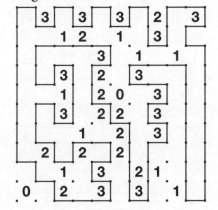

Page 220

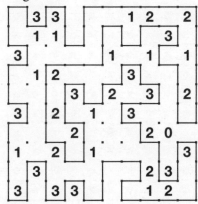

Page 221

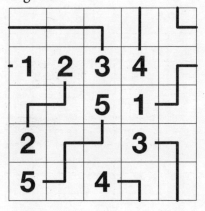

Page 222

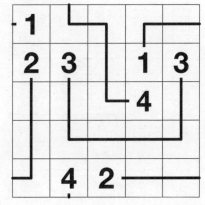

SOLUTIONS

Page 223

Page 224

O	O	X	X	O	O	O	X	O	X
X	O	O	O	X	X	X	O	O	O
X	O	X	X	X	O	O	X	X	X
X	X	X	O	X	X	X	O	X	O
O	O	O	X	O	X	X	O	X	O
O	X	X	X	O	X	O	O	O	X
O	O	O	X	X	O	X	O	X	O
X	X	X	O	X	X	O	X	X	O
X	X	O	X	O	O	O	X	O	X
O	X	X	O	O	X	O	O	X	O

Page 225

X	O	X	X	X	O	X	O	O	O
O	O	X	O	X	X	O	X	O	X
O	X	O	O	O	X	O	X	X	O
O	O	X	O	X	X	O	O	X	O
X	O	X	X	X	O	X	O	O	X
O	O	O	X	O	O	O	X	X	X
O	X	O	X	O	O	O	X	O	X
X	X	O	O	X	X	O	O	X	O
O	O	X	X	X	O	X	X	X	O
O	O	X	O	X	X	O	X	O	X

Page 235

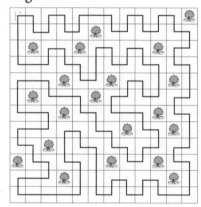

Page 236

Page 237

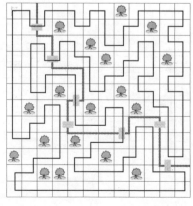

SOLUTIONS

Page 238

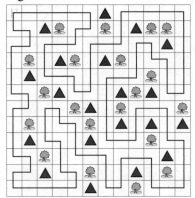

Page 239

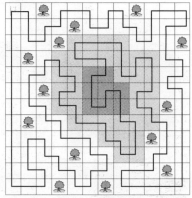

Page 240

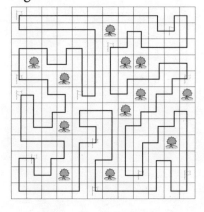

Page 241

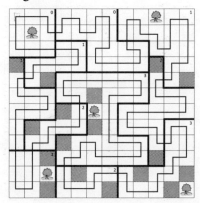

Page 251

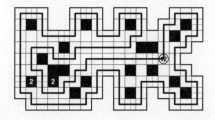

Page 252

20	20	20	20	20	20	20	4	4	4	1	4
3	3	20	3	3	3	20	4	5	5	4	4
1	3	20	20	5	5	20	5	5	2	2	4
3	2	2	20	1	5	20	20	5	3	4	5
3	3	20	20	5	5	14	14	3	3	4	5
5	5	20	4	4	4	14	2	2	4	4	5
5	1	20	14	1	4	14	3	3	3	5	5
5	5	20	14	14	14	14	14	14	14	14	14

SOLUTIONS

Page 253

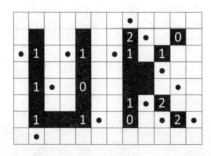

Page 254

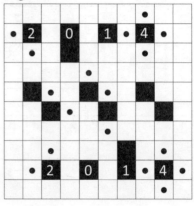

Page 255

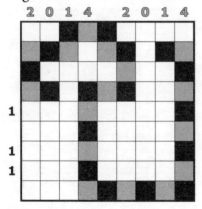

Page 256

Page 257

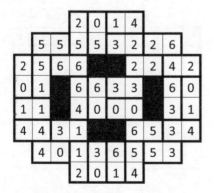

Page 258

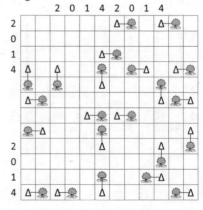

SOLUTIONS

Page 259

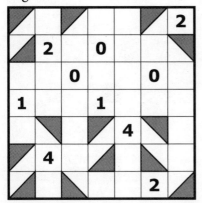

Page 260

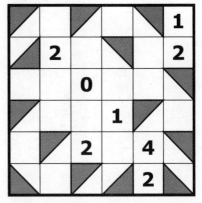

Page 261

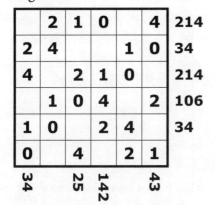

Page 262

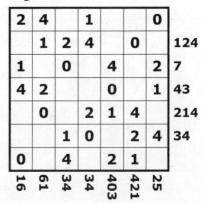

Page 263

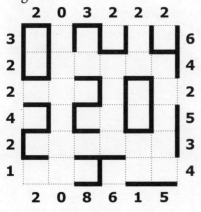

Page 264

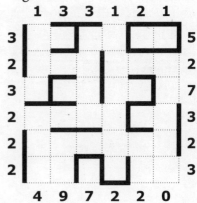

SOLUTIONS

Page 265

```
                                          K
      M   H   S                   A   E
  S H A K A S H A K A             R   I
      S   S   I                   U   S
      Y   H   K                   K   U
    N U R I K A B E               O   K
          W   K           K   E N K E N
  S       O   U           A   E
  K R O P K I             K               F
  Y       A       F       U       K       O
  S U D O K U     S U R A R O M U         U
  C       E       T       O       R       R
  R       R       O           P   O       W
  A   A   O       S           U   D       I
  P   K           H           Z   O       N
H E Y A W A K E   I           Z   K       D
  R   R           K       C L O U D S
  S L I T H E R L I N K       E
```

READY TO QUALIFY?

Enjoyed the puzzles in this book and think you could qualify for the next World Puzzle Championship?

British solvers should visit www.ukpuzzles.org for details of qualifying competitions, and also see the introduction on pages 13 to 14. Those not eligible for the UK team should instead visit the World Puzzle Federation (WPF) website at www.worldpuzzle.org and use the 'Members' link to find the 'WPF Members' page. Choose your country to view details of your local organisation, and get in touch. Or, if your country is not listed, you can contact the WPF directly using the contact details listed on the site.

FROM THE SAME AUTHOR

The Mammoth Book of Brain Games

Includes some types of puzzle similar to those found in this book

One Year To A Better Brain!

A fun programme featuring LOGIC, OBSERVATION, NUMBER, WORD puzzles and more

78 entirely different types of puzzle

52 weeks of daily content

Features over 300 puzzles, all created especially for this book, plus weekly
'Re-Thinking' pages that feature a range of suggestions and ideas to help
improve your memory and unleash your creativity, challenging
you to make better use of your brain in your daily life.

A scoring system helps to keep you motivated as you improve week by week, with the
final page of each week's puzzle offering you the chance to find your BRAIN RANK.

Visit www.littlebrown.co.uk for more information

FROM THE SAME AUTHOR

The Mammoth Book of New Sudoku

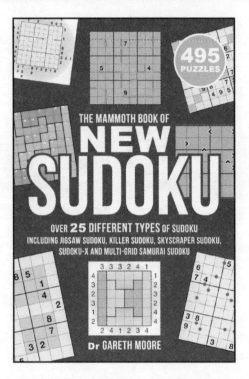

Contains many of the puzzles you would find in the annual World Sudoku Championship

Much more than just a puzzle book

A comprehensive collection featuring every significant variant ever created

Over 25 major Sudoku types

Nearly 150 different variants

Almost 500 puzzles, all created especially for this book, including Jigsaw Sudoku, Killer Sudoku and multi-grid Samurai Sudoku

No other collection of Sudoku comes close – this is without doubt the most definitive volume of Sudoku variants ever compiled, with full instructions and solutions included throughout.

Visit www.littlebrown.co.uk for more information

FROM THE SAME AUTHOR
The Mindfulness Puzzle Books

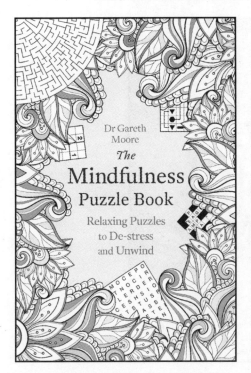

A mix of relaxing puzzles to solve during a coffee break

Three volumes now available

Best-selling puzzle master Dr Gareth Moore has compiled these three volumes of specially selected puzzles to provide the perfect level of challenge and reward for your brain, helping you to relax and helping to inspire creativity.

Feel the tension release as you focus on each achievable and fun task, and experience the endorphin reward buzz as you successfully complete each puzzle. Stimulating your mind with each puzzle helps unlock your brain's innate creativity, and this book will help you feel refreshed and renewed, and ready to carry on with your daily life.

The contents of each volume includes a wide selection of standard puzzle types, avoiding the stress of the new, but without the boredom of over-repetition. They also include adult versions of relaxing kids' activities, such as dot-to-dots, mazes and even colouring and spot-the-difference puzzles.

Visit www.littlebrown.co.uk for more information.

FROM THE SAME AUTHOR

The Mammoth Book of Logical Brain Games

Packed with similar types of puzzle to those found in this book

The world's most comprehensive collection of logical puzzles

More than **440** puzzles

Over **60** different types of puzzle

Covering all major types of logic puzzle, this book has everything from Sudoku and Kakuro through to Hanjie and Slitherlink, plus a whole lot more besides such as Tapa, Fences, Yajilin, Nurikabe, Fillomino and many, many others. All of the puzzles use pure logic, requiring no language or cultural knowledge to solve, so the book is suitable for everyone.

Fun and addictive, these puzzles offer a fantastic mental workout. Each of the more than 60 types of puzzle is presented with full instructions in seven carefully graded difficulty levels, from Beginner right through to Master, so whatever your experience you'll find perfect challenge.

Visit www.littlebrown.co.uk for more information.